MW00532542

This signed edition of

ALL THE TIME IN THE WORLD

by

JOHN GIERACH

has been specially bound by the publisher.

ALSO BY JOHN GIERACH

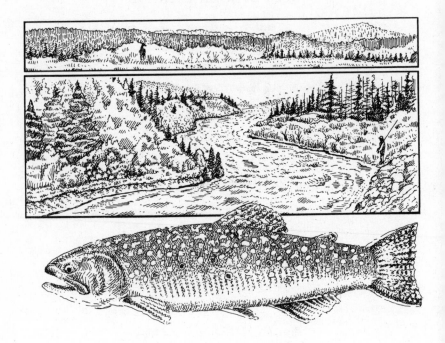

ALL THE TIME IN THE WORLD

JOHN GIERACH

Art by Glenn Wolff

Simon & Schuster

NEW YORK LONDON TORONTO
SYDNEY NEW DELHI

Simon & Schuster
1230 Avenue of the Americas
New York, NY 10020

Copyright © 2023 by John Gierach

All rights reserved, including the right to reproduce this book
or portions thereof in any form whatsoever. For information,
address Simon & Schuster Subsidiary Rights Department,
1230 Avenue of the Americas, New York, NY 10020.

First Simon & Schuster hardcover edition March 2023

SIMON & SCHUSTER and colophon are registered trademarks
of Simon & Schuster, Inc.

For information about special discounts for bulk purchases,
please contact Simon & Schuster Special Sales at 1-866-506-1949
or business@simonandschuster.com.

The Simon & Schuster Speakers Bureau can bring authors to your
live event. For more information or to book an event, contact the
Simon & Schuster Speakers Bureau at 1-866-248-3049
or visit our website at www.simonspeakers.com.

Manufactured in the United States of America

10 9 8 7 6 5 4 3 2 1

Library of Congress Cataloging-in-Publication Data has been applied for.

ISBN 978-1-5011-6865-9
ISBN 978-1-5011-6866-6 (ebook)

The fishermen have the fastest boats of all. Their boats scarcely touch the water. They have much equipment, thousands of dollars worth. They can't fish in one place for fear that there are more fish in another place.

—WENDELL BERRY

CONTENTS

ALL THE TIME
IN THE WORLD

1

FISHERMEN ARE EVERYWHERE

Fishermen are everywhere; all it takes is for the subject to come up, and somehow it always does. I had a plumber out the other day to look at my clogged toilet. When I explained that the plunger had no effect, he smiled in the kindly way of a doctor comforting a worried parent and said that yes, he'd seen this before, it wasn't terminal and he knew just what to do. But then on his way to the bathroom, he stopped to look at the fish photos I have tacked up in my office.

"You like to fly-fish," he said. "I'm an ice fisherman myself . . ." and we were off to the races.

Not long before that, my firewood guy, Fred, was out making a delivery and as we unloaded two cords of dry pine he explained to me, as he always does, how many more trout I'd catch if I'd only use live bait. Fred thinks I fish with artificial flies because I'm squeamish about worms and he is only trying to be helpful, but of course, he's wasting his time. People fish the way they want to and won't be talked out of it. After you've explained in detail how your method is better than theirs in every conceivable way, they'll smile benignly and say, "Well, this is just how I like to do it," and you can't argue with that.

Once I was in northern Michigan fishing with a friend, a local who seemed to know every sweet spot in the county as well as every year-round resident of his hometown of Charlevoix. One afternoon, we stopped at the docks to see how the weigh-in for the Trout Tournament was going and ran into a guy my friend had known since grade school. We told him we'd been out fly-fishing the local rivers and he said, "I thought about getting into fly-fishing once, but it's too expensive."

My friend and I exchanged a look. This guy had just stepped off a cabin cruiser suitable for the high seas of Lake Michigan, with twin 50-horse outboards, military-grade fish-finding electronics, and enough tackle to stock a Bass Pro Shop that, all together, must have set him back six figures. We could have explained how much fly-fishing that kind of money could buy, but at the moment the guy couldn't have been happier with things as they were. He'd just brought in a 30-pound chinook that he thought might land him first place in the salmon category, which would be worth a thousand dollars in prize money, a mount of the fish by a good local taxidermist, and a place in local history. So we wished him luck with his fish, grabbed dinner at a café, and then headed off to catch the evening hatch.

When I took up fly-fishing in the late 1960s, I was naturally lumped in with the influx of hippies who'd recently adopted the sport and who were held responsible for techniques that were considered heresies then, but have since become standard practice. I can't say it was a bum rap because I looked and sometimes acted the part, but in fact I was never entirely successful as a hippie. I believed in peace, love, and the simple life in a general way, and still do, but my redneck streak ran deep and the yin-and-yang symbol you saw everywhere then as an emblem of balance and harmony always reminded me of two pork chops in a frying pan.

And I wasn't much interested in heresy, either. Early on I fell in with a crowd that favored the bamboo rods and hackled dry flies that were already beginning to look dated by the early '70s. Maybe we'd turned our backs on so much of our buttoned-down upbringing that we were attracted to this harmless backwater of sporting tradition as a kind of security blanket, or maybe we just understood that those guys had been at this for a while and knew things we didn't. Whatever the reason, we imagined ourselves to be the counterculture equivalent of tweedy sportsmen, while the old-timers just saw us as a bunch of charm school dropouts who needed haircuts.

It could have been another phase I was going through—we all went through some phases back then—but that vision of the sport took hold as just the way I like to do it, although that's not to say I've never strayed.

Most of my flies are tied from drab natural materials in the old Catskill style, but I also like to have a few of the latest cartoon-colored plastic and rubber monstrosities and I'm not above tying one on when I think it'll outperform fur and feathers.

Most of my favorite rods are still bamboo—old tackle triggers the kind of nostalgia that's irresistible to some—but I fish some graphites, too, including a few that are among the best fly rods I've ever cast, as well as some others that make me wonder what I was thinking at the time.

I've fished with spinning rods, but not often. It's not that I have anything against them, but that I somehow went from the level-wind bait casters of my youth straight to fly rods without that intermediate step. I must have missed the whole spin fishing thing while I was away at college.

And I've fished my share of bait. There were the worms I drowned as a kid, as well as red wigglers and live hoppers I sometimes fished with a fly rod on days when I wanted dinner and proper dry flies weren't producing. I've thought about revealing my secret history as a worm-dunker to Fred, but by now the whole bait/fly controversy has become a private joke that we both enjoy.

I was down at our little market in town recently and a fly fisherman who works there told me he was taking up ice fishing this year as a way to while away the off season. (Ice fishing again; it must be in the air.) I almost gave him my old ice auger, but then thought better of it. I haven't ice fished in twenty years, but I still have the auger and the guy had a point: winters here are uneventful enough that sitting out on the ice staring down a hole—"the stone-age equivalent of watching television," as Jim Harrison called it—could begin to look pretty entertaining.

I find it comfortable and comforting to live in a place like this that's not a big fishing destination, but where fishing is just an ordinary thing people do when they have the time, or, in some cases, go to considerable trouble to *make* the time. Where the guy behind the counter at the feed store—standing under a mount of a 30-pound lake trout—asks if you've been getting out without having to specify out where and doing what. (I've noticed that 30 pounds is about the minimum size for mounting a lake trout. It must be some kind of unwritten rule.)

But I also love the expeditions, especially those that take me to places you could call wilderness if only because you won't see anyone on the water that you didn't see at breakfast. Sometimes the fish there are bigger and more numerous than you're used to; other times they just haven't yet been made hysterical by a constant barrage of flies. Or maybe they've seen their share of plugs and spinners, but are pushovers for the feathery liveliness of streamers, making you look like a better fisherman than you are.

In the end, though, it's all just fishing and therefore better some days than others. But even when the catching is slow there are compensations, like a sense of scale and emptiness you won't find on your neighborhood creeks and, once the droning of the outboard and the small talk go silent, a kind of sublime stillness. It's one thing to not hear any traffic noise, but another altogether to know that the nearest automobile is a hundred miles away by floatplane.

Or maybe you bump into some local wildlife—woodland caribou, let's say—and rather than running in terror at the sight of a human, they just stand there as dumbfounded as dairy cows, while you think, *I am a long way from home.*

I do know how I like to fish—with floating lines and dry flies as a benchmark, followed closely by dries and droppers, swung wet flies, and streamers—all methods that were familiar a century ago. But I also know that the quickest way to get off on the wrong foot is to show up thinking you know better than the guides who've worked their water for years. Even on days when the guide is clearly guessing, I have to think his guess is better than mine and I've learned a lot just by following instructions.

Sometimes it's something new, like the flapdoodle, a quick and dirty way to attach a barrel swivel and spinner blade to an otherwise conventional salmon fly. This rig sinks the fly deeper and adds a mechanical flash that can sometimes open the mouths of recalcitrant king salmon. (And if hardware is too nontraditional for your sensibilities, I can show you hundred-year-old tackle catalogs offering flies fitted with blades and propellers as evidence that our grandfathers weren't as stodgy as we thought.) Honestly, I was skeptical myself at first, but I was fishing a flapdoodle behind a 5/0 pink bunny fly when I cracked 30 pounds on king salmon, so I came around pretty quickly.

More often, though, it's just a new fly pattern or some nuance of drift or a counterintuitive mend in the line; something so close to what I'd been doing all along that it was almost indistinguishable, but still just different enough to make a difference. These are the things you learn incrementally, but that accumulate over time into something like instinct.

It took me a while—probably too long—but even when the fishing is good, I now like to stop casting occasionally just to look around; not to bag snaps to post on Facebook, but to form memories in the old, manual way that gave rise to the phrase "the picture doesn't do it justice." After all, it's less about the fish themselves than about the unlikely and often beautiful places we go to find them as well as the time-consuming slog of getting there in the first place. And if nothing else, when someone asks what the place was like, it's nice to have an answer.

Most guides understand a little sightseeing and leave you to it, while others—often the youngest ones—freak out, thinking you're either bored or that you're having a stroke, and stopping to explain yourself has a way of ruining the moment. It's best if you can arrange to wander off by yourself for a while (travel writer Paul Theroux once wrote, "As soon as I was alone I could think straight") but guides don't like to leave their charges unsupervised because God knows what kind of trouble they could get into. Fishing guides sit up late some nights swapping stories about their hapless clients and the idiotic mistakes they make.

The same thing goes when I'm back in camp. Given the interminable chores, demanding logistics, and a revolving crop of new and often clueless fishermen every week, it's amazing that these places run as smoothly as they usually do. It's even more amazing that, even in close quarters, most of the work goes on behind the scenes, where you never see it. So, although I might feel like a frontiersman when I come in off the water to build a warming fire in my cabin, I'll remind myself that it was someone else who cut and split the wood and stacked it on the porch. I spent too many years doing other people's dirty work to ever take for granted those who now do it for me and it's one more thing to think about when it's time to ante up my tip.

Once, not that long ago, contact with the outside world was not only all but unheard-of at these remote fishing camps, it was something to be dreaded. Case in point: it was over thirty years ago now that I was sitting at the dinner table at a fly-in lodge in northern Canada when the cook came in, put her hand on the shoulder of a man sitting across from me, and said, "You have a call."

The table went silent. Forks froze halfway to mouths. In those days, a "call" meant that someone was trying to reach you on the shortwave radio that could be heard crackling and spitting in the kitchen like electronic bacon—our only tenuous link to civilization—and since it's only bad news that can't wait till you get home, you imagine the worst: accidents, house fires, death . . .

But this time it was only business—something urgent at the man's law firm. We could overhear Lorraine, the lodge owner's wife, a hundred fifty kilometers away in Goose Bay, saying she had his partners on the phone from LA and was prepared to relay the conversation. Shouting in order to be heard over the static, our colleague said, "LORRAINE! TELL THEM I'M *FISHING*!"

It was a good answer and should have been the end of it, but it wasn't. The man stayed on the radio for quite a while, but we'd stopped eavesdropping and gone back to chattering about the day's fishing. Compared to real disaster, a problem at work was too mundane to hold our interest. The poor guy finally came back to the table half an hour later, looking exasperated and followed by the cook, who'd spirited his dinner away to keep it warm in the oven until he was ready for it. "Bless her heart," as my grandmother would have said.

Some people think being this profoundly out of touch is dangerous. They're probably right, but forget that it's no more dangerous than driving to the store for a quart of milk. My father used to have a plaque over his desk at work that read "Illigitimus non carborundum," Latin for "Don't let the bastards grind you down," and although he didn't live to ever fish at a place this remote, he'd have savored the idea that in a fishing camp the bastards not only couldn't grind him down but probably couldn't even reach him.

Sadly, more and more of these camps now have Wi-Fi reception, so instead of lounging and talking in the evenings, fishermen rush off to check emails from work or learn about their kids' soccer games, and that old sense of timeless isolation has been lost. It would be easy enough to turn everything off and get it back, but no one ever does.

The sport *has* changed and any of us who thought it wouldn't were being naïve. (We changed it ourselves when we took it up in our twenties and thirties. That's why the old guys kept giving us the hairy eyeball.) And that fisherman in Michigan was right: it's gotten more expensive. A few weeks ago, a friend sent me a new, high-tech leader nipper that retails for seventy dollars, or nearly three times what I paid for my first fly rod. I wondered if this was an example of inflation or a sign of what's happening to the sport, but decided it was the latter because you can still buy the traditional leader nipper—a pair of fingernail clippers—for the price of a cup of coffee.

Something else that didn't cost much was my rubber snake. It's a pretty convincing facsimile of a coiled rattlesnake, thirteen inches across and not quite as big around as my wrist, with its rattle elevated menacingly and its mouth open to expose rubber fangs. This is rattlesnake country, so it gave me a good start when I saw it at a yard sale, coiled on a card table amid the screwdrivers and coffee cups, and as soon as I recovered, the twelve-year-old boy who still lives inside me had to have it.

At the time, some of us belonged to a fishing lease on a trout stream in Wyoming—an ordinary freestone creek made better because only a handful of us ever fished it. The catch was, the place was said to be lousy with rattlesnakes, and because some members brought their kids and dogs there, we were asked to carry sidearms and dispatch any rattlers we saw. I was skeptical of the stories. In the years I fished there, the only snakes I ever saw were harmless bull snakes or plains garters. But I nonetheless loaded my dad's old revolver with snake shot and dutifully carried it every time I fished there.

It also happened that one of the people I fished the lease with had a thing about rattlesnakes. I don't mean the healthy respect we all have, but something approaching a phobia that made him twitchy at the thought of them and caused him to jump at things like the clicking of grasshoppers in the weeds. He was the one guy in the group who didn't carry a sidearm, but the sight of the rest of us strapping on our six-guns every morning must have kept the whole snake business fresh in his mind.

Now, I've never been a big practical joker, but as the new owner of a realistic rubber rattlesnake, the obvious gag suggested itself. So, I brought the snake along the next time we fished the lease and waited for my chance to plant it in the trail ahead of my victim, or maybe just plop it outside his tent, where it would be the first thing he saw in the morning.

But as I waited for my opportunity, I started to stew about it. The trouble with practical jokes is that if they fall flat, you not only look like a fool, but tempt revenge just for the lame attempt, while if they're successful, they demand serious payback, and the more successful they are, the more diabolical and unexpected that payback will be. For that matter, the meanness of playing on someone's weakness that you thought would be funny might feel creepy after the fact, or maybe the inherent cruelty that made it seem like a good prank in the first place ends up revealing something about you that you'd rather not have widely known. And they've been known to go terribly wrong: maybe someone falls and breaks a leg or, God forbid, has a heart attack.

At a certain age, you've made so many dumb mistakes that you're able to identify the kind of faulty thinking that leads up to them, so after carrying the snake around in my pack for a day and a half, I finally stuffed it under the seat of my pickup and abandoned the plan. And then an odd thing happened. Up till then I'd been fishing poorly—pooching easy casts, missing strikes, breaking off fish—but once that stupid snake was out of the picture, I began to fish brilliantly and ended up catching the largest trout I ever landed there: a big fat brown that measured so close to 18 inches that I forgave myself the offending fraction of an inch, as any fisherman would have.

We eventually dropped out of that lease for reasons I no longer remember—time passes; things change. The rubber snake now sits coiled in a corner of my office on top of my old Remington typewriter as a reminder of that brown trout, what led up to it, and that although fishing is no longer really about success, catching fish is still somehow right at the heart of the game.

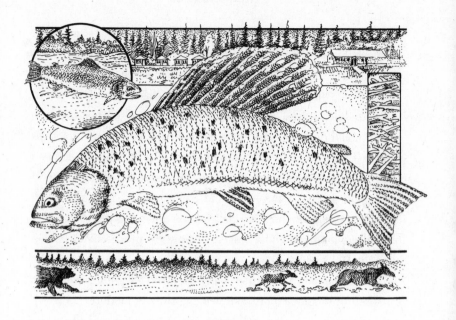

2

ANIAK

I flew from Denver to Anchorage to meet my friend Mike Dvorak, who'd come up from Minneapolis. This was on the afternoon of the summer solstice: the longest day and shortest night of the year, which at that latitude amounts to a few dusky hours, but no real night at all, and I was already anticipating the disorienting effects of nonstop daylight. It's not so much the sleep deprivation as that the boundaries between days dissolve, leaving you with the sense that something has gone haywire with time itself.

We spent what passed for the night in a motel near the airport and flew out to Aniak the next morning on a regional airline. Our

11

flight left an hour and a half late—about par for Alaska—and when we finally boarded, the pilot said, "Sorry for the delay. We had to go through three aircraft, but now I think we've got a good one."

Aniak is one of those outpost towns that haven't bothered to pretty themselves up for tourists. ATVs and outboards were disassembled on lawns with their parts spread out on tarps; pickups were left with their hoods yawning open like patients in dentist's chairs; a leaning shed was propped up with a spruce pole; and an odd assortment of dogs lounged around looking bored and disheveled. No rustic bistros; no shops selling trinkets, and in this proudly mixed-race village the high school basketball team has provocatively named itself the Halfbreeds.

The terminal at the airport was a quonset hut populated by the usual mix of itinerant sports and working stiffs. A medium-sized dog with a dirty face wandered through the sparse crowd—yellow Lab and pit bull, if I had to guess. Word is she lived nearby and met every flight, working the crowd for handouts like a Southern politician. Once we met the guides and collected our gear, we were escorted outside to the lodge van, an old yellow school bus with a transmission that sounded like a coffee grinder.

We met the camp manager, Ludi Gericke, at the office of the Aniak River Lodge, where he held court in his South African accent with a husky named Oakley at his feet. Ludi manages the business of the camp from town, where there's at least spotty cell phone and Wi-Fi coverage, and he explained why the same signals upriver at the camp were even less reliable, as if our main concern was signal strength rather than the quality of the fishing. It was too technical to follow, but sounded vaguely like the old party line telephones from the 1950s that wouldn't let you make a call if your neighbor was already talking. I didn't mention that I'd turned off my phone and wouldn't turn it on again until I got back to Anchorage. When I started coming north in simpler times, I wasn't kidding when I told people I'd be out of touch until I got home, and although that's now changing in some places, I'm sticking to my story.

From there we piled into a johnboat with Aaron, the head guide, motored up the Kuskokwim River for a mile or so, and turned south into the Aniak, where we stopped to try for a pod of sheefish that were rolling in a trough along the east bank. "Aniak" is a Yup'ik word meaning something like "where it comes in," referring to the mouth of a river, or exactly where we were at the moment.

Sheefish are large members of the whitefish family with bass-like mouths and silhouettes that resemble tarpon. They're good to eat, but they don't freeze well for shipping, so few outside Alaska have ever tasted one. Some who write about Alaskan fishing claim that they're known as "the tarpon of the north," but no one actually calls them that. They call them sheefish. We swung streamers to cruising fish and in an hour of blind casting, Mike picked up a small one and then a bruiser about 34 inches long, while I couldn't buy a take. By way of consolation, Aaron assured me they were notoriously hard to catch.

After a twenty-five-mile run upriver to the camp, we tossed our gear in one of the cabins and sat down to supper with the guides at the lodge. The room was large and sparsely furnished, with the regulation picture windows overlooking the river. The walls were nearly bare except for the mounted head of a bull moose gazing down on the table like a huge dog waiting for a handout. This was the first week the camp was open and Mike and I were the only fishermen. We joked about being props in a dress rehearsal for the real clients, but in fact we had the unheard-of luxury of fresh guides and a whole river all to ourselves.

The next morning, we went out again with Aaron and swung pink bunny flies for chum salmon in a run where they're known to pod up.

Fish were rolling when we got there, but when we began hooking up they turned out to be kings weighing between 10 and 12 pounds. The catch was that the king salmon run in the Aniak was so skimpy that year that Alaska Fish & Game had closed the season on them. The rules were specific: we weren't supposed to knowingly target kings, but if we hooked one inadvertently we could land it (or try to), but we couldn't keep it or lift it from the water for any reason. So that's what we did, but after a couple of fish each we could no longer maintain the fantasy that we were fishing for chums and getting kings by mistake, so we reeled in and went looking for rainbows.

Early in the season, rainbows are usually found in the spectacular logjams this river piles up as it changes course at will in the spring floods, washing away entire trees in the process. Some old jams are left dry and bleached on sandbars where the water once flowed, while the fresher ones are piled in the river with the current bulging against them, sometimes with leaves and needles still attached. Other trees lie with their crowns snagged in midriver and their exposed root balls bobbing rhythmically in the current like trolls shaking their fists at the sky. There's so much wood in this river that Ludi had warned us in advance not to bring sinking lines. "All you'll do is lose flies," he said.

We ended up snaking some fat rainbows out of the wood on weighted streamers after giving foam and deer hair mice a good try. Mice are usually the hot ticket here early in the season, but Aaron thought the rainbows weren't on them yet because the river was still too high and dark. Maybe the fish couldn't even see our flies on the surface, or maybe they could but they were too much trouble to go after in the fast water. I thought it might be the unusually hot weather. (I'd packed fleece, wool, and rain gear for the Alaska I remembered, but was fishing in shirtsleeves with my nose peeling from sunburn.) But the real reason was that we had outsmarted ourselves by coming early to beat the rush on the mousing and getting there *too* early. It's the oldest story in fishing.

The next day we went out with Tristan and tried the king spot again. Salmon running to spawn are forever shuffling upstream and we hoped the kings had moved out and been replaced by chums. In fact, the kings from the day before *had* moved out and were replaced by larger kings. We caught a few to make sure. Mike's best weighed about 20 pounds and it was that rosy pink color they begin to turn when they enter fresh water. That color change is the first outward sign that the fish is dying, as all Pacific salmon do after they spawn. It's like leaves turning colors in October before they fall off the tree and just as poignantly pretty, so Mike, a photographer by trade, took a few photos while Tristan held the fish carefully (and legally) in the water.

We never saw my biggest. It nearly yanked the rod from my hand when it hit and then bore off unstoppably for 30 or 40 yards before the hook came loose. As I was reeling in, Mike said, "I wish you could see your face." I can imagine: heartbroken over losing a fish I knew I shouldn't have hooked in the first place. Kings are my favorite salmon, but even on a vacant river where bumping into a ranger is unlikely, the honor system is still binding.

So we motored up a clear tributary called the Buckstock and caught grayling. I've had a soft spot for arctic grayling ever since I caught them forty years ago in the Northwest Territories on my first junket as a writer. With their iridescent bodies, prissy little mouths designed for eating insects, and that flamboyantly tall dorsal fin with its pink and lavender spots, they wouldn't look out of place on a coral reef. I've since caught Montana grayling in some of the mountain lakes in the Rockies where they've been stocked, but Michigan grayling were already a fading memory long before I ever fished there, the victims of overfishing, trout stocking, and logging. If you say Michigan grayling now, people might think you mean Grayling, Michigan, a village of fewer than 2,000 residents, some of whom don't realize that their town is named after a locally extinct fish.

I've never found grayling to be difficult to catch, but their best waters are so remote that just getting to where the fish are is plenty hard enough. The grayling in the Buckstock ranged from 15 inches up to a few that were pushing 20 and they'd ignore a size 12 dry fly on a dead drift, but eat it happily if you gave it a little upstream twitch as it came into their window. They were lovely fish and I had my little waterproof digital camera with me, but Mike is a photographer whose work hangs in museums, so I left the picture taking to him. He'd lift a fish from the water, gently jiggle it once so it would elevate that big fin the way we'd throw out our arms to keep our balance, snap the photo, and have the fish back in the water in three seconds. Mike has been at this a long time and knows all the tricks.

On the way out, we fished a slot right on the mud line where the clear Buckstock entered the cloudier Aniak, trying for a small pod of chums. The chums were having none of it, but we got some of the Dolly Vardens, grayling, and rainbows that were dogging the spawning salmon hoping for a meal of eggs. We also spotted a big, solitary king—a pink slab that might have gone 30 pounds—but we left it alone.

After a few more days we moved another fifteen miles upriver to a tent camp. The place was presided over by a caretaker named Mike Monroe, known affectionately to the guides as Uncle Fucker. He spends the entire season up there, mostly alone with his two black Labs, Rio and G.B., and, for two days each week, either welcomes or tolerates fishermen; it's hard to tell which. His legendary grumpiness may just be an act, as some claim, but if it is, it's an award-winning performance.

Mike and I went out every day with two 8-weight rods each, one rigged with a mouse, the other with a streamer. Now and then the odd rainbow would tumble for the mouse, but we were pulling them out of the logjams on streamers on a fairly regular basis. They were lovely big fish with deep green backs, wide crimson stripes, pearl-colored bellies, and ink-black spots that extended all the way to their lips and dribbled down their pectoral fins like coarsely ground pepper.

These are resident rainbows that feed on rodents and fish in the early season, and then for the next few months, as five species of salmon successively enter the river to spawn and then die, on salmon eggs in the millions, followed by tons of the decaying flesh of the salmon themselves. These fish don't have to go to sea like steelhead to get fat because the sea conveniently comes to them.

I don't think a day went by when we didn't see moose, including several cows with twin calves. Mike and I never saw a bear, but two of the other guides did. A cow moose and two calves ran headlong across the river in front of them with a brown bear in pursuit, closing on the baby that was lagging behind, but when the bear spotted the boat it veered off and retreated. (Bears are hunted here, so they're shy of humans.) Your sympathy naturally lies with the calf, with its knobby knees and Bullwinkle face, but we reminded ourselves that nothing eats if nothing dies and that the bear was hungry and may have had cubs to feed.

The river in this upper stretch is inscrutably braided with dead-end side channels and tributaries, and we were happy to be with guides who knew where they were going. On your own, it would be too easy to go up a feeder creek thinking you were still in the river and end up God knows where. It happens. New guides sometimes get lost in this maze and there's the story of a party of fishermen from the town of Aniak that blasted up a tributary creek thinking they were still in the river and, miles up in there, finally ran their jet boat aground at full speed, wrecking their craft and losing most of their gear.

With no other option, they started the long hike out, but making your way through these scrubby, tangled northern forests isn't like strolling in a park. Bears are built like tanks and moose are up on stilts, but humans crash and stumble and don't make much headway, so after several grueling days they'd managed to go only a few miles.

These guys had two strokes of luck: one was that they'd retrieved their flare gun; the other was they were smart enough not to use it until they heard a distant outboard passing on the river. That was a guide on his way back to camp after a day of fishing. The flare was barely visible over the treetops, but from its position it was obvious where they must be. They were a mess, as you'd expect: tired, hungry, wet, exhausted, covered with mosquito bites, and borderline hysterical.

The way the guides tell it, these guys were hapless idiots, but then there are two unwritten rules in operation here. One is that if someone is in trouble, you're obliged to drop everything and help; the other states that once you've rescued someone, you've earned the right to make fun of them.

One day at a place called Timber Creek, we beached our boat near the mouth of the stream and hiked upstream for a while before fishing back down. Mike went ahead with our guide Ron, fishing a mouse, while I came along fifty yards behind with a weighted streamer called a Slump Buster.

We got several nice rainbows, and after we'd gone a quarter mile or so, Mike and Ron spotted a big one—even at a distance their body language was unmistakable—and Mike ran the mouse over it a dozen times without a look. Finally, they waved me down, pointed out where the fish was, and stood back for me to make the cast.

The fish took on the first swing and the fight seemed to last forever as it tried its best to tangle me in the logjams that clog this little river. Every time it made a dash for cover, I put the brakes on—hoping for the best and fearing the worst—and every time the leader ticked a snag, my breath caught and my heart stopped. This wasn't a marginally legal king salmon, but a big rainbow I had every right to if I could manage to land it, which I somehow eventually did. It was the only fish we measured on that trip: 25 inches long and so fat I could barely get my hands around it to pose for the photo. I could go on about it, as fishermen do, but let's just say that bigger and possibly even prettier rainbows have been caught in Alaska, but not by me.

After I released it, I furled my fly and followed Ron and Mike as they fished on down to the boat. They didn't have to ask why I'd stopped casting. This was near the end of what seemed like a week-long, sleepless blur of fish and it must have been obvious that I was experiencing a kind of bliss, a term Paul Theroux once defined as "the exalted state of not wishing to be anywhere else."

Back at camp, Uncle Fucker and I sat by the fire he'd built—not for warmth, because it was hot, but to discourage the swarms of mosquitos—and talked about how, as the permafrost melts from the effects of global warming, it spits up mammoth teeth and farts ancient trapped methane into the atmosphere, a greenhouse gas that only makes matters worse. He said that in recent years he's watched the once-permanent snowfields in the Kuskokwim Mountains forty miles away shrink inexorably until they're now half the size they were just a few seasons ago. I felt I was beginning to locate the source of the grouchiness. Many of us wonder what the world will look like in another twenty years, but few have a front porch view of receding glaciers or the days of solitude to contemplate what they mean.

I couldn't help thinking about all the fossil fuel I'd burned recently. A pickup truck to the airport parking lot, shuttle bus to the terminal, two airplanes to Aniak, and then all the way upriver in a johnboat with a 40-horse outboard and a gas tank the size of a steamer trunk, all to arrive in the wilderness to commiserate with Uncle F. about the effects of climate change. Something else to keep me awake at night, as if the midnight sun weren't enough.

From there on out it was all the tedious anticlimax of travel: one more night at the main lodge, then the long boat ride to the ramshackle airport in Aniak and the uneventful flight back to Anchorage, where the temperature was a record-breaking 90 degrees and the air was smoky from wildfires. The first thing I saw when we walked into the terminal was an overheated family of four sitting side by side on a bench with their mouths open like a school of carp. That night we ate dinner at a restaurant overlooking the seaplane base at Lake Spenard. The place had huge picture windows so we tourists could sit and watch the planes come and go as if they were some species of endangered waterfowl.

On the walk between the restaurant and our motel, we had to stop and wait at a traffic light and there in the heat and bustle of the biggest city in the state it was hard to believe that just that morning we'd been on a river still wild enough that you can catch all the fish you want without being much of a fisherman, so bragging is pointless, although most of us do it anyway. So in spite of everything, maybe Alaska really is "The Last Frontier," as its license plates proclaim, conjuring up all the lopsided romance, thoughtless rapacity, and cracker barrel humor that phrase implies.

I remember that when the territory gained statehood in 1959 a series of dumb jokes made the rounds about how Texas, at half the size of Alaska, was no longer the biggest state in the union. In one, an insecure Texan strolls into a hardware store in Anchorage, kicks a roll of fencing, and says, "Our chickens back home would walk right through this stuff," and the clerk replies, "That ain't chicken wire, mister; it's mosquito netting."

3

DRY FLIES

The timing of a fishing trip is always such a crapshoot, especially when you're hoping to fish dry flies. The character of previous months, the seasonal but not quite predictable emergence of aquatic insects, and the moment-to-moment clockwork of weather all have to dovetail in particular ways for things to work out. And this all has to happen at a time when the rest of your life lets you blow town for a few days. Wendell Berry said that certainty is so rare we must learn to act decisively in ignorance. Ed Zern said, "The best time to go fishing is when you can."

We went to the river a few weeks earlier than usual, in late April instead of early May, or toward what would normally be the hesitant beginnings of the hatches rather than later, when they'd be thicker and more dependable. We were worried about that year's high snowpack, which could force dam managers to dump water into the river early to make room for the extra runoff that would soon spill uncontrollably into the reservoir. Like all rivers, there's a volume of water here above which fishing a dry fly becomes pointless unless you're trying to win a bet. You may not have a specific number of cubic feet per second in mind, but you'll know it when you see it—and we've all seen it.

These hatches, if they came off, would be blue-wing Olive mayflies, possibly with a smattering of early Pale Morning Duns, plus caddis flies and assorted midges, all in hook sizes 16 through 22 except for some of the midges, which can be vanishingly small. We all have the flies and all but one of us also carry magnifier glasses so we can see to tie them on.

There are always a few die-hard fishermen on the water here, but it was still cold in the mornings, so instead of getting out early, most were having leisurely café breakfasts followed by second and third cups of coffee; definitely up for it, but in no hurry. There'd been a quick blizzard the day before we drove over from the east slope of the mountains—the kind of dense spring snow that shovels like cement—but by the time we got going the next day the roads were just wet with a little ice left on the passes, while the storm itself had blown toward Nebraska and points east.

We spread out on a stretch of river where the trout are known to rise freely if there's any reason to and staked out spots to wait for the hatch. Of course, we all know how to nymph fish and one of us (not me) is good enough at it to teach classes in the technique, but when we come to fish dry flies we get single-minded about it. There were four of us that week, all old enough to remember when nymph fishing as we now know it, with strike indicators and added weight on the leader, was frowned upon. But it was our generation that took nymphing from something a respectable fly fisherman just didn't do, to something a respectable fly fisherman didn't do in front of witnesses, to a minor tactic that was good for a few extra trout between rises, to a method so effective that some saw no reason to fish any other way.

But for most of us it's the sheer beauty of fishing dry flies that's irresistible—the sip of a fly off the surface, the head-and-tail roll, the occasional explosion, and the heart-stopping refusal rise that elevates your dry fly on a little clear bump of water a split second after the fish has already vanished. It's said that trout only do about 20 percent of their feeding at the surface, but the percentage of flies for sale that are designed either to float outright or drift so shallowly that you can see the swirls when trout take them is closer to 50 percent and well-known rivers still get crowded when hatches are due. For most, dry fly fishing is somewhere between a preference and a self-imposed limitation and if nothing else, fly rods are at their best when casting unweighted flies with tapered leaders and floating lines. It's true that an adequate fly caster can effectively honk out weighted nymph rigs all day long, but the inherent elegance of the instrument is lost.

Sometimes it's a practical matter. Many of the streams in northern Michigan are so jumbled with sunken timber that it's impossible to fish under the surface for more than a few casts without losing your nymphs, and you'll even lose dry flies to snags you thought were deep enough to clear the hook point, but weren't. A fly shop owner in Boyne City told me about a guy from out of town who said he was there to nymph the Jordan River, which is one of the stickiest streams in the region. The owner explained the situation, but his customer said that although that might be a problem for

23

some, he was a "competitive nymph fisherman" and didn't expect any problems.

The next morning the guy was back in the shop. To his credit, he opened with, "Okay, you were right; I was wrong. Can ya help me pick out some dry flies?"

I've always thought that the sport's origin story was all about floating flies. Archaeologists say the earliest fishhooks they've found —made of shell—are 20,000 years old, which means we were fishing with hook and line 15,000 years before we developed settled agriculture. The rod would have come along as soon as it was necessary because even a chimpanzee knows that if he needs extra reach, all he has to do is get a stick.

One of the earliest descriptions of actual fly-fishing is in *De Natura Animalium*, written in the third century AD by Claudius Aelianus, who wrote about "certain spotted fishes" that ate insects "which fly about the river" and "float on the top of the water." But the flies themselves were too fragile to use as bait, so local fishermen attached colored wool and rooster feathers to their hooks and caught the fish that way. That sounds like match-the-hatch dry fly fishing to me, although none of this had yet evolved into the modern niceties of sport. This was just human ingenuity addressing the need for something to eat.

So we spread out along the river—three out of four of us within sight of each other—and stood there scanning the water for whatever was there to see. You go down a checklist from the obvious to the obscure. First you look for the rings of rising trout in all the usual places and strain to see infinitesimal wing pairs on the water or the specks of flies in the air. Then you push your vision through the surface as much as water clarity, available light, and your eyesight will allow, looking for any sign from the fish that a hatch is beginning.

I always have trouble spotting trout in the water unless they're doing something, like flashing down deep to take nymphs or, better yet, suspending closer to the surface to pick off emerging insects. Sometimes I'll see trout that aren't there. A tumbling submerged leaf easily becomes a brown trout elevating to eat a nymph and ripples in the current distort bottom rocks and shadows in convincingly trout-like ways. In extreme cases, I've spent time casting to trout that weren't actually trout and then tried to act nonchalant about it when I realized my mistake. This tendency we have to impose meaningful patterns on random objects is known to psychologists as pareidolia. It's the same thing that allows some people to see the face of Jesus toasted onto an English muffin.

My mind does wander after a while when I'm watching a river— sometimes to the weirdest places—and when it comes back I may find myself staring uncomprehendingly at a rising trout. When that happens I can only wonder, *Where was I and how long was I gone?*

This river is known for its multiple hatches that sputter on and off early in the season. There'll be a fifteen-minute pulse of flies, a flurry of rises, and then you're back to gazing at the water again, listening to the wind, water, and scattered birdsongs that pass for silence here. It's easy to waste time changing flies, and knowing you don't have forever to get it done only makes you clumsier, so the one thing we listen to on our obligatory stop at the local fly shop is what the predominant hatch of the moment is. Of course, as out-of-towners we always get the full rundown on the river from a clerk in his twenties or thirties. Sometimes one of us points out that we were fishing here before he was born, which he takes to mean that we know things that are no longer true.

Otherwise, we've got this trip down pat after decades of repeat performances. We go almost every spring and usually again in the fall for what we've come to think of as the first and last dry fly fishing of the season. We drive over by the same route, stay in the same motel, go to the same fly shop, where the people and the dogs remember us, and in the evenings we eat supper in the bars. One of us no longer drinks at all and the other three can now go for days between beers, but now that the town has become gentrified, the real restaurants are too expensive and the only other choice is the microwave over at the 7-Eleven.

Once we've fished for a day or two we begin to get our own sense of what the hatches are doing, so I'll wait for the rise to begin with a brace of flies already tied on. One is always a size 20 Blue-wing Olive parachute and the other could be anything from a small caddis, to a midge, to a low-floating sprout emerger, to the latest miracle pattern I sprang for at the shop, but one fly is always a Pale Morning Dun if any of them have been seen around. According to the hatch charts, this mayfly isn't supposed to be on this early, but sometimes a few of them dribble off anyway and the trout here have a sweet tooth for them. If there are two dozen Olives on the water and one Pale Morning Dun, the trout will eat the PMD.

One afternoon, Ed and I were standing below a good riffle waiting for rises when a nymph fisherman in his twenties came hurrying downriver. He asked me if I could spare him some 6X tippet, which he promptly dropped and lost in the tall grass, so I cut him another piece, automatically checking my spool to see how much I had left. He asked us about fly patterns, where to fish on the river, where we were from, how many split shot to use, how we liked our rods, what kind of bird that was, what time of day was best, and so on. We told him what we could, but both had the feeling that the answers weren't really sinking in.

Before he left—taking his nervous energy with him—he gave us one last puzzled look, as if the inefficiency of just standing there when we could have been carpet-bombing the river with split shot struck him as vaguely un-American. Later Ed said he thought the kid was playing dumb—either mining us for information or waiting us out for our spot—while I thought he was legitimately in the dark, although we both agreed that cannabis may have been involved. There's a look of distracted focus (or is it focused distraction?) that you come to recognize, especially if it's a look you once regularly wore yourself.

Of course, it's all perfectly legal here in Colorado now, but even back in my misdemeanor pot smoking days I never could fish stoned and didn't see why you'd want to. I've long since quit, but I voted for legalization on the libertarian premise that people should be able to do what they want as long as it doesn't hurt anyone.

When we got home a few days later I found that I'd left my pickup parked under a tree that a flock of wild turkeys had been roosting in, so my vehicle was covered in a week's worth of shit, some still fresh, some dried to the consistency of plaster. Now, I'm not normally one to wash cars—I figure it'll rain eventually—but this time I drove straight to the coin-op car wash in town and spent a double handful of quarters scrubbing the thing off. It cleaned up real nice.

As it turned out, we'd made the right call. The hatches had come off sporadically, we'd caught at least some fish every day on dry flies, and not long after we left they did, in fact, blow up the flow, cancelling the rest of the river's early dry fly fishing. But the following week I couldn't resist driving up to our local tailwater—which has the advantage of being a thirty-minute drive from home instead of five hours—to see what was going on. It was seven days closer to being the right time for an Olive hatch, and although we had a pretty high snowpack on our own side of the Continental Divide and the freestone streams were already beginning to blow out, the flow out of the dam was still fishably low.

There were fishermen in the first few places I looked at as I drove down the canyon road; singles and pairs, all apparently casting unweighted flies. So the good news was, word was out that something was happening on the river, while the bad news was, word was out that something was happening.

I was halfway down the canyon before I found an unoccupied run, and even before I got in the water I could see scattered rises and some small mayflies in the air that had to be Blue-wing Olives. Some fishermen step into a situation like this thinking, *Okay, these fish are toast*—I know that because I've actually heard it said—but even after four decades of fly-fishing I experience something like stage fright. Everyone has bad days—usually without advance warning—and every time I step into a trout stream I wonder if this is one of them.

But the trout were rising freely and it was an easy run, with long, uniform currents that made for good drifts, so I did okay. That is, I missed fish in the usual ways—bad casts, dragged flies, premature hook sets—but also hooked and landed more than I missed. After I'd fished up into the riffle at the head of the pool, I got out and moseyed back down to the bottom for another pass. By then my incipient case of the yips had been replaced by a sense of absolution and I fished well, picking up a few more trout. I didn't tune in the news on the drive home, so as not to spoil the mood.

A week later I was back with my friend Vince. They'd bumped the flow by a few more cubic feet per second, but the river was still in decent shape and it was a perfect day for a hatch: chilly, darkly overcast, and threatening rain. There was some urgency. These tailwaters with their controlled flows are the last to hold out in the spring, and we knew that once they blew up, fishing would be off for no less than six weeks.

The river was a little more crowded this time and guides had appeared with their long-handled landing nets and clients in tow. So we shot for a place we know: a side channel with a deep run that can't be seen from the road. It's not exactly a secret pool (there are no secrets left on these popular rivers) but it *is* overlooked by some, and by the time we got there, mayflies were coming off nicely and trout were rising. It's a small spot, so we traded off strike for strike, getting some easy fish out in the main current and then trying for the harder ones tucked in the slower backwater, tight to the far bank.

We had good fishing for a few hours before it started to rain. At first it was just a sprinkle that didn't bother us or the fish, but pretty soon it was coming down hard enough to put off the hatch, so we walked back to Vince's truck. By the time we got there it was pouring rain and starting to hail, so we stashed our rods in the rod caddy and bolted for the cab with hailstones landing around us like mortar shells.

It went on to hail violently for the next twenty minutes, sounding like ballpeen hammer blows on the cab. It was too loud to talk, so Vince just looked at me and grinned. This was a new truck, but he'd gotten it for $22,000 off the list price because it had been damaged on the lot by a previous hailstorm. It was a screaming deal and he said that after a week or so he didn't even notice the dents anymore.

That much hail does to a river what ice cubes do to a gin and tonic, so the water would be too cold for a hatch until tomorrow. When it finally let up we drove slowly back up the canyon toward the coffee shop in town in four-wheel drive, skidding at anything over 15 miles an hour on the three inches of ball bearing–sized hailstones on the road. We passed one rental car that had slid into the ditch (if they'd gone off the other side they'd have landed in the river) and dodged another rental flying down the canyon at about triple the safe speed.

It's easy to spot the tourists here, not only by their lack of mountain driving skills, but because Colorado issues its rental car plates with the numbers and the trademark silhouette of mountains in fire engine red on white instead of the resident green. They do that so we locals will know who to watch out for.

4

THE GREEN CABIN

Two friends had planned to meet me on the river, but they bailed at the last minute owing to an unscheduled conference call for one and broken-down equipment for the other. This has happened before with these two. In the world where they make their livelihoods, going fishing isn't considered an excused absence, although you can sometimes finesse it by vaguely saying you'll be "out of town that day." (We're all convinced that there was once a time when we could go fishing whenever we felt like it, but none of us can put a finger on exactly when that time was.) I was sorry they couldn't make it—anyone you'd call a friend is, by definition, a pleasure to fish with—but by midafternoon I was thinking, *I'm glad those guys didn't show up, so I don't have to share this.*

The spot I picked was first shown to me years ago by the guy with the conference call and it quickly became a favorite. It's a broad, shallow glide where the river breaks into braided channels snaking through softer water—an ornate maze of current that seems specifically designed to flummox fishermen. It can be lousy with trout, but it seems like no matter what you do, the leader drags, the flies skate, and the low, clear water forces you to stand back and make the kind of long casts that only magnify the problem. And in this long-standing catch-and-release water, the trout have seen it all, so they'll flush if you do the least little thing wrong. I *am* sometimes capable of fishing brilliantly in conditions this difficult, but it's not a superpower I can depend on. In my case, brilliance arrives as unpredictably as a lightning strike and lasts about as long.

The sweet spot here is up at the head of this run, where the current that feeds the braids resolves into a deeper, narrower slot. When a hatch is on, trout will usually stack up in here, rising in the main current and sometimes in the eddies along the rocky far bank. The casting here isn't easy, but it's a relief from the puzzle downstream by at least being difficult in a more straightforward way. At the head of this slot is a small, rocky island held in place by the roots of a dense stand of willow saplings and below it, where the twin channels of the river reconverge, there's an eddy where the right cast with the rod held high will leave a dry fly drifting in a continuous, loopy circle until your outstretched arm begins to quiver.

That eddy and the slot below are the prime feeding lies and the trout are often larger here than in the braids below, so this is where I like to end up. I fish this stretch of river the same way I used to do my homework—*when* I did my homework—by wading through the hardest part first and leaving the easy part to look forward to.

The difference between the two was illustrated by the results of my college entrance exams—a primitive form of the SATs. I scored in the 90s in language and humanities and barely registered in math and science, foreshadowing a future where I'd write books for a living, but be unable to add two numbers together without a calculator.

At the top of this run I'll get up on the bank to take a break. By then a few hours have gone by and it's all been so engrossing that this is the first time I might spare a thought for whatever had to be left undone that day so I could go fishing, as well as for "absent friends," as the poignant old toast goes. From this vantage point, I have a clear view of a slick on the far side of the island where fish sometimes feed. To get over there, I have to wade the near channel with its fast current and slick rocks, but sometimes it's worth doing. I've never been a strong wader, but my estimation of where I can cross a river has always depended on whether or not I see trout rising on the other side.

I'll also check back downstream to see if fish have started feeding in the braids again. If they have, I might slip back into the water and fish back down, but only after changing out the flies I used on the first pass. My thinking is that even though the fish have been rested, they've seen those flies once today and might still be leery of them. This is either a well-thought-out tactic or a way to justify all the patterns I carry for these small hatches. I'll either dead-drift my flies on a downstream cast or switch to a brace of wet flies and swing as if I were fishing for salmon. I imagine that I base the choice on the way the fish are behaving, but it probably has more to do with the mood I'm in.

On some unpredictable days when the fishing has been good, it will all seem so self-contained at that point that I'll reel in, walk back to the truck, and drive home, maybe with a stop at the fly shop in the small town at the head of the canyon to chew the fat for half an hour. I used to fish "ferociously," as Russell Chatham once said, and walking away from rising fish was an acquired taste, but I've since come to like the idea of catching a few, but otherwise leaving things the way I found them, with the fish still going about their daily business of getting enough to eat.

There's a cabin on the far bank of this run that I've always liked. It's a small, frame place with a porch overlooking the river, a chimney and wind cap for a woodstove, and at least half a dozen bird feeders: a blue-collar cabin reminiscent of the days when an ordinary working stiff could still afford a little place on the water. It's painted a kind of pea-soup green and so many other cabins in the canyon are one faded shade or another of that same color that there must have once been a big sale on the paint. I've never seen anyone there because I fish the river early and late in the season to avoid the worst of the crowds—before the summer people arrive and after they've left—but the firewood pile grows and shrinks seasonally to show that the place isn't abandoned, and sometimes in October I'll see a lone mountain chickadee perched on an empty feeder, wondering what happened to his free lunch.

There's another good run upstream that's also associated with a cabin. We call that one the Asshole's Pool after the landowner, who has a long-standing bone to pick with fishermen and doesn't have bird feeders, probably because he thinks the birds are trespassing. We haven't named this first one. We still refer to it clumsily as "not the Asshole's Pool, but the other one with the cabin." The shorthand that would normally make this the Cabin Pool hasn't kicked in yet and the names of pools and riffles have to be left to arise naturally because when they're forced, they end up sounding as soulless as streets in a subdivision.

The day I'm remembering was in late April, usually a good time for pre-runoff fishing, but that year the spring storms had been scarce and a stretch of bright, dry weather had kept the hatches sparse and the fish spooky. But then here came a big, slow-moving front with the gray sky, drizzle, chilly air, and falling barometer that make for heavier hatches and hungrier trout—and my friends couldn't make it. Tough luck, guys. I'll let you know how it went.

I thought I saw trout rising as I was walking up to the braids from downstream, but I couldn't be sure until I waded in and had a closer look. The quiet dimples of fish feeding on small insects in elaborate currents can be hard to spot from a distance, and when you want them to be there it's easy to imagine them. But no, there they were, the barely discernible rings of feeding trout that deformed and washed away downstream in a heartbeat or two. The bugs were the usual suspects for April: small Olive mayflies and even smaller midges. By squinting hard, I could just make out some of the miniature sail-like wings of mayflies on the water, while the midges were smaller specks in the air above the river, outnumbering the mayflies three or four to one.

I don't remember what flies I tied on, but I'm a creature of habit, so it's a fair bet it was my old standard size 20 parachute with a smaller nondescript nymph on a dropper, squeezed wet before the first cast to make it drift just below the surface. Then I'd have glanced at the sky to reassure myself that my beneficial overcast wasn't breaking up, and checked for an escape route in case there was a flash flood. In this spot that route is a notch to the east of the green cabin that's not quite as steep as the surrounding canyon wall.

Flash floods do happen here. Since I've lived in the area there have been two in this canyon alone. The so-called thousand-year flood in 2013 was plenty bad enough, with eight deaths and millions of dollars in damage to roads and cabins, but it was the freak storm in 1976 that everyone here who's old enough still remembers. That summer an epic thunderstorm dropped three-quarters of our average year's rainfall at the head of the drainage in four hours, caus-ing what's been called a "wall of water"—but was probably more like a wedge—that sluiced down the canyon and killed 143 people, some of whom were never found. (That number was revised years later when a man who'd been listed as missing and presumed dead was found to be living in Oklahoma.) There were dozens of harrowing stories, but the upshot was that those who climbed the canyon wall stood a better chance than those who tried to drive out. I was in the canyon myself that day, but the fishing was poor and, like our friend from Oklahoma, I left early, thereby buying myself another forty-five years on earth along with everything that came with it.

The year of that flood, I'd just bought a house on another river, where I'd live for the next twenty-one years. It was a luxury to string up a rod at home and walk to the water, but in high-runoff years I worried about flooding, and not without reason. There were no outward signs on the house, but in the crawl space underneath where I went often to fiddle with my troublesome water pump, there was still a watermark from an old flood from before my time that the previous owner hadn't bothered to mention.

I liked having a river for a neighbor, as any fisherman would, but it wasn't as idyllic as it sounds. This wasn't much of a house to begin with and by the end of my tenure it was old, leaky, and drafty, with faulty plumbing, heating, and wiring; it was listing slightly eastward with the prevailing wind and had warped and settled so that doors and windows either wouldn't open or wouldn't close. In short, it was falling to pieces in every imaginable way and wasn't worth saving even for sentimental reasons. So, when the time came, I wasn't sorry to sell out and move away or to see the house bulldozed. (I'd fantasized about bulldozing it myself.) My only regret was that they cut down the huge old elm tree that once shaded the porch.

That place was long gone by the 2013 flood, but if it had still been standing, the water would have been waist-deep in the kitchen and the whole place might have washed off its sandstone foundation and crumpled to rubble, as other houses in the valley did. Now I live a few miles away on a saddle between two creek drainages where the water would have to rise a hundred feet to reach my door. At the time, it was just the right house at the right price, but later I wondered if the location was an example of my Midwestern tendency to keep even the things I love at arm's length. You do what you can to hedge your bets, but it usually just comes down to luck. We can spend our lives thinking we're successfully dodging bullets, when in most cases the bullets simply weren't aimed at us in the first place.

So my warm feelings about that green cabin in the canyon come less from wishing I owned it and more from thinking, without much evidence, that I'd like the people who do. The place is well kept up, but unpretentious in a lived-in sort of way, and I imagine the owners as lean, gray-haired bird-watchers waving from the porch and calling, "Hey, how's the fishin'?"

I caught some fish in the braids that day. Not a lot in the grand scheme of trout fishing, but a lot from a place that's more likely than not to leave me scratching my head. It was still spring, but I'd been out enough to shake off most of my off-season cobwebs, and I had the advantage of skanky weather and trout that seemed as happy as I was to finally see a heavy hatch of bugs. But even then, as I'd study a spot trying to work out the precise angle of cast and mend that would give me six inches of drift, I'd lose the thread momentarily and remember my late poet friend Jack Collom saying of current that "the bumps remain even as the water moves on by," or Jim Harrison writing, "Moving water is forever in the present tense, a condition we rather achingly avoid."

I don't know how long I spent in the braids—fishing time isn't measured in the conventional way—but the hatch was still going when I reached the channel above, with mayflies now outnumbering the midges. A few trout were sipping in the softer eddies on the far side and in the main current some fish were leaving quiet rings while others were rolling at the surface, showing their heads and dorsal fins in quick succession with a little flip at the end as if they were wagging their tails happily. The phrase "innocent victims" flashed through my mind in a predatory way.

I got my first few trout on the dry fly, so I took a minute to nip off the dropper so I wouldn't accidentally foul-hook a fish on that second fly. That does happen, and although it doesn't necessarily ruin things, it does put a kink in the sloppy perfection of a good day, especially when it's a nice fish that you'd have preferred either to hook and land fairly or miss altogether.

Up till then I'd gotten all brown trout—the predominant species in this river—but then halfway up the channel I hooked a heavier fish that pulled the slack line from my left hand and briefly got on the reel. A minute later, when I turned him out of the current, I could see this was a nice rainbow; not huge, but thick and beautifully colored with a wide red stripe, deep green back shading to silvery olive flanks, and black spots like splattered ink.

Rainbows are prized on this river, so I got it in mind to hand-land the fish and get a picture of it with my cell phone, as I'd seen others do so easily. But I'd never actually tried it before and found that juggling a fly rod, cell phone, and wiggling fish can go terribly wrong. The best I can say is that when it was over the fish went back in the river and somehow the phone didn't. I've always liked fishing alone and one reason is that when things spiral into this kind of slapstick comedy, at least there are no witnesses.

I got a few more browns from the slot and then put a dozen good drifts in the eddy below the island, but there were either no fish there, or at least none that were interested in my fly. So, I got up on the bank in my usual spot for my usual break. There were two or three trout dimpling in the slick up by the island and a few more working down in the braids, but it was now late in the hatch, things were clearly winding down, so this seemed like the right time to stop. I might have hooked another trout or two before it was all over, but why take the edge off a good day by scrambling to run up the score at the last minute?

Also, for that matter, I was wet. The drizzle that day wasn't much more than a cold mist, but over the last few hours it had gradually defeated my miracle-fiber jacket in a real-time demonstration of the difference between "water resistant" and "water*proof*." I remembered a friend from Maine once asking me, "What is it with you guys from Colorado that makes you want to get wet first and *then* put on your raincoat?"

I clipped off my bedraggled but still usable fly and put it back in the box where it belonged, then reeled in and walked back downstream to my truck. I knew I wasn't required to text my friends a fishing report, but now that we have the technology, it's half-expected and they'd be curious to know what they missed. My plan had been to send them the snapshot of that rainbow without further comment, but a picture is worth a thousand words only if you manage to bag the shot.

So, as I drove toward town, where I'd pass through a few blocks' worth of cell signal on my way home, I tried to compose the single short sentence that would hint at the fishing and poke a little fun at my friends for not being there, because they'd expect no less. Brevity is the soul of texting, and if I could come up with just the right sentence, one would be enough. As Hemingway said, a story is always better the more you can leave out of it.

5

LICENSES

I don't remember when I started saving my old fishing licenses. All I know is that at some point, instead of throwing them away, I began stuffing the expired ones into a manila envelope that has now grown to the thickness of a hardback novel. Even in my busiest seasons I only accumulate five or six permits a year, so I must have been doing this for quite a while now.

I also don't know why, since I have no plans ever to do anything with them, although I did get a fleeting idea when I saw a large walnut-framed display on the wall of my insurance agent's office. It was a black-and-white snapshot of his late father as a young man—holding a large trout and grinning maniacally—surrounded by a lifetime's worth of Colorado resident fishing licenses.

Does that mean he never fished anywhere else? I didn't ask, but—not to sound like the chamber of commerce or anything—it would be possible to happily fly-fish for trout here for your whole life without ever leaving the state, especially if you started in the 1920s, like he did.

I briefly flirted with doing something like that, but realized that although it was a fitting tribute to a deceased father, constructing that kind of monument to myself would amount to a monstrous act of vanity that I'd come to regret. So I wrote it off as just one more example of someone getting sentimental about old licenses, and here's another:

A neighbor who was moving away from the area came to my door one day carrying the mounted head of a three-point mule deer buck with a license glued to the back that was dated 1925. The story is that it was a local ranch kid's first deer, and although the head wasn't impressive, the kid's proud father had it mounted anyway to commemorate the event. The trophy was given away when the family left the area and has since been passed around locally in order to keep it in the valley, where it belongs. Did I want to become its new caretaker? Of course I did; I'm a sucker for this kind of thing and my neighbor knew it.

I hung the little buck in a back corner of my office next to the bathroom, where he seems to be peeking out from behind a tall bookcase—not exactly a place of honor, but a place nonetheless. In the years since, the glass eyes have clouded over, one ear has begun to droop in a dog-like way, and every time I try to dust it, some hair comes out. It wasn't the highest quality mount to begin with and it's now just shy of a hundred years old. I'm not sure what I'll do with it when the time comes, but I'm not gonna be the one who throws it away.

I grew up fishing with my father and a favorite uncle, but I don't have my first license and in fact have no memory at all of fishing licenses from my childhood. I *can* say that if I'd needed a license, my straitlaced father would have made sure I had one, but that my uncle, who came from what I affectionately think of as the hillbilly side of the family, considered things like season dates, bag limits, and fishing licenses to be pointless formalities. As I said, I don't remember. Anyway, I was underage and therefore not legally responsible—a state of grace I probably didn't fully appreciate at the time.

I've never gone without a fishing license as an adult, but I did once leave it at home and that was naturally one of the few times I've ever been checked by a game warden. The law here says that you have to have your license on you, but the warden gave me a break. Instead of writing me up on the spot, he gave me his card and told me to mail him a photocopy of my license, which had the date and time of purchase stamped on it so he'd know I bought it before, not after, he stopped me. So, no harm done, but I still remember that claustrophobic sense of getting nabbed and I didn't like it.

I like to think I've retained some of the natural anarchy of youth that my black sheep uncle encouraged, but, like my father, I'm careful to obey the fishing laws and I always have a license. It's the right thing to do and, if nothing else, it's easier on the nerves. Mark Twain wrote that if you tell the truth, you're not always trying to remember what you said. Likewise, if you don't break the rules, you don't have to keep looking over your shoulder.

A warden I used to know was well aware of that. Most game wardens are beleaguered, with too much territory to cover and more violators than they could ever apprehend, but this guy said he saved time by not bothering to check fishermen he knew were legal.

"How can you tell?" I asked.

"Oh," he said, "I can spot a law-abiding fisherman by his body language when he sees me coming and by the quality of his tackle." That may sound elitist, but it stands to reason that a guy who'll spend a thousand dollars on fishing gear will spring for a few extra bucks for a license.

He went on to say that although some wardens eventually got cynical, he was still entertained by the lame excuses people came up with when they were forced to improvise on the spot. Apparently "I have a license, but I left it at home" is as venerable a classic as "The dog ate my homework."

We've all bumped into perpetrators from time to time and they always see themselves as justified. I once met a man who was walking away from a river with more than his legal limit of trout on a stringer. When I asked about it, he said the way he figured it, if the limit was eight trout per day (as it was then) but the last time out he hadn't caught any, then this time he was entitled to keep sixteen. I wanted to tell him it didn't work that way, but he knew that. He was just trying out his defense on an objective observer.

A man once told me that he never bothered to buy a fishing license because he only fished a day or two every year when his grandson came to visit and it just wasn't worth the expense. I told him that if he got busted it would cost him a lot more than a license. He said, "Yeah, but I've never gotten busted," and I didn't know what to say to that. It would be impossible to accurately calculate your chances of getting popped, but with wardens spread as thinly as they usually are, your odds of committing the perfect crime are probably fairly good.

Once I was fishing the San Juan River in New Mexico near the spot where the regulations changed from catch and release to a slot limit. I'd taken a seat on the bank to rebuild my leader and change my fly when I noticed an older guy on the far side of the river wading downstream in knee-deep water. He was dragging his right leg along in what looked like a painful limp and I thought, *Good for you, man. Still out here fishing even with a bum leg.* But then once he got down below the catch-and-release sign, he looked around to see if anyone was watching (he must not have seen me sitting there), then reached down, unhooked the stringer he had tied to his ankle, and lifted out two 16-inch rainbows. He fastened the stringer to his belt and waded on downstream without a trace of a limp. I know what he was thinking: that twenty yards one side or the other of a sign amounts to a mere technicality. I'll admit to having mixed feelings. One side of me recognized him for the cheat that he was, while the other side wanted at least to award him a point or two for ingenuity.

Back in the early 1970s I went to a hippie wedding in the mountains near here where the happy couple was "hitched" after a fashion, though maybe not strictly according to Colorado law. After the ceremony, the groom told me they were serving lunch at the outdoor reception, adding, "You'll like it; we're having trout." When I moseyed over to the grill to have a look I found no less than fifty fresh brook trout neatly laid out on a picnic table.

"Where'd these fish come from?" I asked, and someone said, "Bob caught 'em yesterday."

With what? I wondered. *A quarter stick of dynamite?*

I knew who Bob was. In another ten years he'd be wearing a coat and tie and driving to work in a late-model Volvo, but for the moment he was a back-to-nature type squatting on public land and imagining himself as a noble savage to whom the rules didn't apply. The Division of Wildlife offered a reward for those who turned in violators—fishermen were worth less than big game hunters, but it was still a tempting bounty—so the question became, Do you call the game warden on a friend's wedding reception? Maybe I should have, but instead I helped myself to a plate of brook trout, baked beans, and potato salad. Does that make me an accomplice?

For some reason, we still often shrug at game violators. We Americans have always admired our outlaws—at least from a safe distance—so maybe we still want the local poacher to be nothing more than a lovable rascal, even though he's really just another petty criminal. Poaching may not actually be a gateway to burglary and mugging, but the motive is the same and real harm is done. I never did find out where Bob got all those brook trout, but I can guarantee you that the fishing there sucked for years to come.

Sometimes you'll stumble into what seem like genuine gray areas. There was once a case here where a fisherman was busted for trespassing for standing in public water but casting upstream onto private. I was especially interested in the outcome of that one because I've done this myself a time or two, assuming that if I didn't literally "set foot" on private water, I was still legal. I didn't know the fisherman in question and all I could learn from some locals I knew was that it was quietly settled out of court and that the landowner was a litigious prick that no one liked.

I once met a man who was fly-fishing a lake that had recently been stocked with hatchery trout. He'd gather a handful of small gravel that he'd then scatter on the water to mimic the fish food these rainbows were used to seeing in the hatchery. Then he'd quickly cast out a size 14 brown nymph that resembled a pellet of Purina Game Fish Chow and wait for the leader to straighten out when a fish took it.

Now, chumming is illegal, but—correct me if I'm wrong—chum has to be edible and gravel isn't, so as I see it this would fall more under the heading of game calling. I talked to the guy when he got out of the water with a couple of trout on a stringer and that's how he saw it, too. He told me the trick was to keep moving because "after a couple of times, the fish figure it out."

When I travel now, I usually buy my out-of-state or out-of-province license online and print it at home—two copies so I can squirrel away a spare in case I lose the one I'm carrying. That's the kind of thing my father would have done. He died long before home computers became ubiquitous and would have thought a website was where a spider decided to set up shop, but if he'd lived he'd have been one of those who backed up his backups.

It's hard to beat the convenience of the electronic transaction, even if the process is sometimes cryptic, but the licenses themselves are disappointing. Fishing licenses have never quite matched the ornate gravitas of stock certificates or currency, but at least they were once printed on waterproof paper, filled out by hand, torn from a book, and stuffed in a pocket-sized license holder with a leaping trout printed on the front along with something like:

Horton's Corner
Chugwater, Wyoming,
Fishing Supplies &
Some Ammunition Available

Now your fishing license is likely to be just one more of the soulless digital printouts that clutter our lives, although I'll admit it's more fun than most.

So although the things we now do online with a few clicks save us time, they also put reality at arm's length, and what are we gonna do with that extra time if not encounter the actual world and the people and things in it? That's why I still prefer buying my license on-site. Sometimes I'll be riding with someone who knows where to go, but just as often I'll be driving alone through unfamiliar territory hoping to spot a fly shop or a general store advertising "gas, worms, and cold beer." Sometimes it's as uninteresting as a stop at the sporting goods counter at a suburban Kmart, but there's always the chance of a good local fly shop or even an old-timey bait store with gurgling minnow tanks and a bench full of geezers drinking coffee out front. Whatever it turns out to be, there's the chance that small talk of the "where you from?" variety will evolve into a useful tip on a place to fish or a good local fly pattern—something that'll never happen on a website.

Once, as a young writer, I went into a fly shop where the clerk recognized my name and said he'd read my book. He didn't say he liked it, just that he'd read it, but I took it as a compliment anyway.

On a drive north from Maine, the friend I was traveling with insisted we get our licenses at a place called Doak's, or the W. W. Doak fly shop, situated in a well-kept Victorian house in, of all places, Doaktown, New Brunswick. This place catered exclusively to fly-fishing for Atlantic salmon, as if no other kind of fishing even existed, and it was everything you could ever hope for: wood-paneled and formal with polished oak bins stocked with thousands of beautifully tied salmon flies and the slightly hushed atmosphere of a museum.

We spent more time there than we'd planned and finally came away with nonresident licenses and handfuls of flies: General Practitioners, Undertakers, Green Machines . . . Then we grabbed coffee to go at Timmy's (Tim Hortons) and drove on toward the Miramichi.

At the other end of the scale, I was fishing warm water in southeastern Kansas—trying to catch longnose gar with a fly rod—and stopped to buy a license at a garage that bore a hand-painted sign proclaiming BAIT.

While the guy filled out my license he launched into a sales pitch for his homemade stink bait, which he sold in unlabeled Mason jars.

He couldn't tell me what was in it—it was a secret family recipe—but he *could* reveal that the final step in preparation was to leave the jars out in the hot sun for a few days to "cure," until the pressure building up inside made the lids pop. He said this stuff was irresistible; that every fisherman in the county swore by it; that it was so effective you could just pour it on the riverbank and collect the catfish as they crawled out of the water to get at it.

He didn't miss a beat when I said I was fly-fishing. "You could scent your flies with it," he said, and I believe he was right. I'd have to look this up to be sure, but I think you could legally scent a fly with stink bait (if "scent" is the right word) and fish it anywhere bait fishing is allowed.

He almost had me sold until he added, "Just be careful to always stay upwind of it, and for Pete's sake don't get any of it on you."

That's when I thanked him and left with my fishing license.

6

ROAD TRIPS

We owe the tradition of the American road trip to Henry Ford and his affordable, mass-produced automobiles that he once said came in any color you wanted as long as it was black. That would include both the idyllic childhood adventures at the lake as well as the nightmares of boredom, trapped in the family station wagon with grumpy parents, your creepy sister, and a carsick dog. But if you're of a certain post–World War II vintage, it was probably Jack Kerouac's 1955 novel, *On the Road*, that put the counterculture romance into the long, aimless drive. Like the one that found me in a borrowed Chevy Impala convertible driving through Georgia sometime in the

1960s with three other long-haired Yankee college students. I don't remember where we were going—if anywhere in particular—but I do remember being pulled over by a couple of large policemen in an otherwise pleasant little one-stop-sign town. We'd been rousted before on this trip and it hadn't always been pleasant, but this time when the driver asked, "What's the trouble, Officer?" one of the cops grinned and said, "No trouble; we just wanted to see if you boys was hippies or werewolves."

And of course, there was fly-fishing, with its built-in belief that the fish were always bigger somewhere else and, furthermore, that the farther you traveled the bigger they'd get. It was an illogical assumption, but how else do you explain someone who settles in Colorado because, among other things, the trout fishing is pretty good, only to end up driving around Wyoming, Idaho, Montana, and Yellowstone National Park to fish rivers that had been written about in books?

I usually went with my friend A.K. in his 352-cubic-inch V-8 Ford pickup with four-on-the-floor and saddle tanks to increase its range. (This was still the era of guilt-free driving with big engines, low mileage, and cheap gas.) We traveled together often in those days and we were an efficient mobile unit with minimal pit stops, no dawdling, and no bickering over finances. Before leaving home, we'd put something like a hundred dollars each in a kitty for shared expenses like campground fees, groceries, and gas. If the kitty ran dry, we'd pony up more money. If there was any left over when we got back, we'd either split it or, if we were feeling flush, find a bar and drink it up. We were both recent transplants to the West, native Midwesterners with the Midwesterner's modest expectations, but we had faith that life, in its fullness, would always provide a few more fish and a little more money—probably never in lavish amounts, but enough of each to keep us going.

We fished the famous rivers we'd read about—plus some not so famous—and met plenty of other starstruck pilgrims with out of state plates. A few of the trout we caught were slightly larger than the ones we got back home, but most weren't. When I mentioned that to Bud Lilly one day on the Lamar River, he said, "Yeah, it's funny. Once the 'experts' started writing about this country, the average fish size increased by a couple of pounds."

It's true that the heart of a trip doesn't depend entirely on its destination, but most of us still need an excuse to overcome inertia and get out the door. Like steelhead, for instance. If you live on the east slope of the northern Colorado Rockies and get a hankering for these sea-run fish, you're faced with—by my calculation—no less than a fifteen-hour drive west and more if you want to get into the good stuff nearer the coast. But of course, with anadromous fish returning from a vast ocean to spawn in their home rivers, the good stuff depends on timing, and when you're coming from elsewhere, timing is a toss-up.

One year a friend and I drove out to fish the Sandy River in Oregon: twenty-three hours on the road, the last few hours of it in the rain. We pulled in the morning after we'd left, checked in at a friend's fly shop for the current fishing report—which wasn't promising—and hit the river.

Long story short, we fished in a downpour for three days. At first we thought nothing of it. We had the right foul-weather gear, and if you don't like fishing in the rain you shouldn't go to the Pacific Northwest in November. We were even cautiously hopeful. After all, steelhead like gloomy weather and sometimes a push of new water will bring more fish into the rivers.

But it kept raining, hard, and the river continued to rise and darken. We spent all day in rain gear, and at night the sound of rain on the roof of the borrowed room above the fly shop lulled us to sleep. We'd long since gone to big, cone-headed flies fished on heavy sinking lines in hopes of reaching down to whatever fish there might have been, but eventually the visibility could be measured in fractions of an inch and it began to look hopeless. I finally lost heart on day three, when I had to reel in to let an entire uprooted cottonwood tree float through the run I was trying to fish. A quick check of the computer at the fly shop revealed that every river in the state was in similar shape and the storm was predicted to get worse, so we turned tail and ran for home.

The storm followed us through parts of five Western states. Mostly it was rain, but we hit snow on Deadman Pass above Pendleton, Oregon, where we followed a snowplow for twenty miles, and again in Utah, just west of the Wyoming line, where it socked in for the duration and slowed us to a crawl. We finally pulled into our hometown in Colorado to radio reports of hazardous driving conditions, school closures, power outages, and cancelled flights at the airport in Denver.

Later, when friends asked how the trip went, we said, "Well, you know, it was steelheading."

The closest to home—and the farthest from salt water—that I ever caught a steelhead was on the Salmon River in Idaho. We were camping and fishing not far upstream from the River of No Return Wilderness, one of the best place-names in the West. There were six fishermen, three trucks, three drift boats, and two dogs and the fishing was slow. Were we too early in the season or too late? Was the run of fish just thin that year or were steelhead already becoming a scarce commodity? It depended on who you asked.

Anyway, by the second to the last day, three of us had landed steelhead and the other three were fishless, but then in midmorning my partner Vince and I beached the boat to swing a good-looking run. We both came up blank and while I was changing out my fly for another pass, Vince walked upstream around a bend to look at the water up there. Shortly thereafter he came trotting downstream with his 14-foot Spey rod bent double on a fish that, once I got it in the net, measured out at a yard long.

Then he led me back and showed me the spot. It was a small eddy that didn't look the least bit fishy except for the rolling backs and dorsal fins of several large steelhead. I hooked up on my third or fourth cast and landed the fish around the bend. It was 30 inches to Vince's 36, but it was a lovely, colored-up hen some nine hundred river miles from the ocean.

That night in camp we learned that one guy, Zak, still hadn't touched a steelhead. We'd been purposely vague about the location of our spot, planning to go back the next day, but Vince gave me a look that seemed to say, "We both know what it's like to be that guy," so the next morning we asked Zak to follow us downriver, pointed out the spot, and left him to it. That night in camp he showed us a digital photo of his steelhead. I was happy for him, but it also occurred to me that I might have caught that fish if I hadn't surprised myself with an act of generosity. A moment of self-discovery. How about that?

We broke camp after breakfast the next morning and planned to drive the whole way home in a single push. But, as often happens now that we're both on the far side of middle age, we ran out of steam by nine o'clock that night and ended up getting a room at Little America, the motel complex on Interstate 80 in Wyoming that's so massive it has its own zip code and glows on the horizon at night like a distant city.

After my first shower in more than a week and a change into clean clothes, I stepped out back for a smoke and found an incongruous couple of acres of lush mown lawn plopped in the middle of thousands of acres of sage. In the dim light of the motel I could make out seven or eight pale shapes roughly the size of soccer balls, which turned out to be fat jackrabbits gorging on this lush grass. Some were so lazy they were lying down to eat; others were upright, but so obese they could barely hop. I thought they'd make a good meal for a coyote, with the added advantage of being not only big and fat, but also slow and easy to catch. For some reason, this little drove of half-tame hares reminded me of that pod of steelhead on the Salmon, although to this day I can't say exactly how.

I live in one of the northernmost counties in Colorado, with Wyoming right over the state line, so my friends and I have spent a fair amount of time up there over the years, even though we don't always get the warmest reception. There's one of those interstate feuds between us that's gone on for so long no one remembers how it started. Folks in Wyoming call Coloradans "Greenies," a reference to the color of our license plates as well as the money we spend on motel rooms, gas, food, and nonresident fishing licenses. They assume we're all well-off, overeducated, and effete and tell jokes that begin with, "How many Coloradoans does it take to screw in a lightbulb?"

I get it. I live a few miles from Rocky Mountain National Park, and although our local economy depends in part on tourism, we're not that thrilled to see the actual tourists. Few of them are as clueless as we make them out to be, but we still can't help lumping them together into a kind of lucrative seasonal infestation.

We used to float the North Platte River in Wyoming every spring and fall when the streamer fishing could be good, at first up near Saratoga, then later on the stretch below Pathfinder Reservoir. One of the features of this river is an infernal upstream wind that picks up in midafternoon and howls until dark. It can be strong enough to blow a drift boat upstream against the current, so the last part of your day is often spent rowing hard downstream in order to make any headway at all against the gale. With this in mind, some locals have mounted outboards on their boats and sometimes one of these rigs would motor past us as we struggled to row into the wind. They'd glance our way and shake their heads at each other, thinking, *Those idiots must be from Colorado.*

I fished for Snake River cutthroats a few times on the north fork of the Tongue River in the Bighorn Mountains in Wyoming. In the stretch I liked, the river meandered through a long, flat bench of land choked with willows and there were good unofficial campsites on a nearby logging road. As well as being lousy with moose, this stretch was also open range for cattle that, by late summer when the fishing was best, had been left alone long enough that they'd turned feral and had essentially become wild animals in spite of the brands on their hips.

One afternoon during a good hatch, I was chased from a pool by a cow moose with a calf. I left willingly, but she shadowed me all the way back to my pickup, making little false charges whenever she spotted me through a break in the willows. I think she wanted to make sure I wasn't just pretending to leave.

So I drove a quarter mile upstream, got back in the river, and was immediately chased by a crazy-looking little range cow that thought I was after *her* calf. She snorted, pawed the ground, and shook her stubby horns as if we were in a bull ring and I was a matador waving a red cape. That night in camp I bragged that I'd not only caught a bunch of trout that day, but had cheated death twice.

It was also in Wyoming—although on a different trip—that I checked into a cheap motel and asked if there were coffeemakers in the rooms, and the desk clerk said, "Well, there's supposed to be, but sometimes the junkies steal 'em."

Now and then on long trips, especially when I'm alone with the tedium of driving, I'll wonder why I'm traveling so far and buying a nonresident license when tourists come every year to fish in my backyard. But as every fisherman knows, sometimes you get a wild hair to do something like catch Yellowstone cutthroats in their namesake river and there's only one place on earth where you can do that. Even if the actuality of it amounts to drudgery, at least the *idea* of a road trip has a restless, literary flavor to it that's irresistible.

Maybe that's why travel writing is such a tempting genre. Life at home seems to trudge along: you make money, spend it, and make more. As soon as you fix one thing, something else breaks. Meanwhile, seasons change, birthdays come and go, and twice a year you reset all the clocks. But a trip has a satisfying beginning, middle, and end and there's a hyperawareness that kicks in, while at home you can spend hours if not days at a time on autopilot. On the road you see new things, meet new people, and have to find your way through unfamiliar territory to end up at a predetermined destination while keeping an eye out for suicidal drivers and avoiding collisions with wildlife. And in the West, with its vast stretches of vacant country, you have to gauge the availability of gas stations and learn to fill up at half a tank, just in case.

And you have to find a place to stay. Once it was a quick roadside camp or just a sleeping bag rolled out in the bed of the pickup to save money, but now that I'm older and more solvent, it's usually the cheapest rented room I can find where I still live out of my duffel, because I won't be there long enough to put things away. The next morning when my travel alarm twitters like an electronic bird, I'll wake up in a strange bed, wondering for a second where I am, and then rustle up the morning coffee—provided the junkies haven't made off with my pot—secure in the knowledge that today won't be the same as yesterday.

Being on the road is a challenge if only because problems arise that you could never have foreseen. For years I had an outdoor sports column at a daily newspaper and sometimes I'd write my stories on the road. This was in the days before computers, cell phones, and email, so I'd bring along a Remington portable typewriter—a sort of primitive laptop—a ream of paper, and some manila envelopes so I could type my column on a picnic table or tailgate, find a post office, and mail it in time to meet my deadline.

But then on one long trip, the fine dust of unpaved roads finally sifted into my typewriter, clogging it beyond repair. It wasn't easy finding a typewriter to borrow, but I eventually located one that had belonged to someone's grandmother. It was an ancient, hulking machine with an ornate script typeface and a red ribbon so old and faded that it printed pink.

The four pages I typed looked embarrassingly garish, but I thought, *Words are words, right?* and mailed it in. By the time I got home and went in to the newsroom, the rumor had already made the rounds that I'd filed a story from a whorehouse in Idaho.

Once I went to Calgary, Alberta, to do a book signing and then go fishing with my guide friend Dave. We floated the nearby Bow River but got tired of dredging nymphs and so Dave asked if I wanted to drive over to the Kootenai River drainage in British Columbia and see about getting some west slope cutthroats on dry flies. He'd never actually been there, but he'd heard tantalizing reports and wanted to check it out.

On the way, we made a short detour to take a look at the Crowsnest River and as we drove over a low bridge, a big, two-inch-long Pteronarcys stone fly landed on the windshield. By the time Dave stopped the truck there were two more and we sat there speechless until a dozen or more of these big flies were crawling on the windshield and hood. Then, still without a word, we parked and strung up our rods. All I had was an old Sofa Pillow left over from Montana and Dave had a couple of size 4 Stimulators with salmon-pink bodies. But they both worked and we caught rainbows until the hatch petered out.

That night we got a room in the nearest town, spent the evening tying more stone flies, and hit the hatch again the next day, catching fish at a steady clip until there were no more flies on the water. Then we drove on over Crowsnest Pass into British Columbia, where we developed car trouble. I don't remember what it was now—maybe the fuel pump or alternator—but we coasted down the pass, limped into a gas station somewhere near Sparwood, and talked to the mechanic on duty. He listened to our amateur diagnosis while wiping his hands on a shop rag and then glanced out at our trailered drift boat.

"Goin' fishin'?" he asked.

"Yup."

"Well then," he said, "I better fix it now."

We did eventually get where we were going and did catch cutthroats on dry flies—big ones, and lots of them. The fishing was so good, in fact, that I ended up going back every few seasons for the next twenty years and Dave eventually moved there. But that's a whole other story.

7

NED'S COVE

I was fishing Ned's Cove on Crossroads Lake in Labrador with Ned himself. It was the third week in August, but that far north it felt more like November: chilly and rainy with a ceiling low enough to ground the floatplane, so instead of flying out for brook trout as usual, we were all out in boats looking for lake trout and pike. Things were winding down. In another week the camp would close for the season.

This lodge has barely been here for a generation, so it's well within living memory that "the cove where Ned found all the lake trout" became Ned's Cove in the same way that "the river over there by the eagle's nest" was shortened for convenience to Eagle River. That nest had blown down in a fierce winter storm before I ever fished there, but from the description I'm guessing it actually belonged to an osprey—a bird known locally as a fish eagle. These place-names are fated to become meaninglessly obscure to those who see them on future maps, but for the time being they still have all their firsthand authority.

I'd never fished with Ned before, but I knew him from previous trips. At first his thick Newfie accent was impenetrable, but with repeated exposure I gradually decoded first phrases, then sentences, and finally entire paragraphs laced with the kind of regional slang that turns an anchor into a "grabble" and an armload of firewood into a "yaffle." So as I zipped up after relieving myself out of the boat that day, I could understand Ned as he began: "Now your men are usually happy to pee over the side like that, but your women, they like to go to shore, where they can have some privacy. But then I had this gal one time who'd just drop 'em and hang it over the gunnel to do her business. Didn't think a thing about it. I seen more of her ass that day than I'd seen of my wife's in five years."

This had been an odd season even for a place where the weather regularly leaves you scratching your head and changing plans. When the crew went in to open the camp that spring, they couldn't land the floatplane because the lake was still frozen and so had to turn around. When they did eventually get in after repeated tries, they spent the first few days shoveling the place out from under six feet of snow, and two days before the first fishermen finally arrived a week late, they pushed the Lund boats across the ice to reach open water.

Once things got under way they found that the big brook trout weren't stacked in the riffles gorging on sucker minnows as usual, because the sucker eggs hadn't hatched yet. Later on, the mayflies and caddis also sputtered off unpredictably. The camp put seventy-eight extra hours of flight time on the de Havilland Beaver and ran the pilot ragged looking for fish, sometimes finding them in the damnedest places and sometimes not finding them at all.

But tales of freaky weather are no longer unique. Half the places I'd been in the last few years had turned out to be freaky hot, cold, wet, dry, windy, or smoky from wildfires. It was starting to sink in that as soon as you ask where you can go to escape the effects of global climate change, the question answers itself.

I stayed in a cabin that week with Tom Rosenbauer from Orvis, whom I'd crossed paths with a few times and knew in passing, and an attorney from North Carolina named Bob Brinson. Tom was there with Colin McKeown and videographer Jeremy Kennedy to shoot an episode of a TV show called *The New Fly Fisher,* which begged the question, what's wrong with the *old* fly fisher?

Bob and I are both repeat clients who came first for the fishing and then returned for more of it, as well as for other reasons that are harder to pin down, but as often as we'd both fished there, we'd never met before. He turned out to be a skilled fisherman and the kind of silver-tongued Southern lawyer you'd love to have on your side in a courtroom, but would dread being cross-examined by. One day he showed me a photo of his bird dogs. With typical legal humor, he'd named these two black Labs Cash and Law.

Fall had set in by late August and the big brook trout were now strung out through the three enormous river systems that give this camp its name, working their way upstream to spawn against a current draining south and east toward the Labrador Sea. It was the only thing that year that happened on schedule. So instead of the concentrations of feeding fish we'd have hoped for earlier in the year, we'd find them in twos and threes if we could find them at all.

Bob and I pounded the two big pools at Vezina Narrows that are usually good for some large fish, but they weren't producing. Our guide, Cliff, kept moving the canoe from one pool to the other as we marched through dry flies, streamers, and nymphs—wringing out the honey holes for all they were worth, but coming up blank. Farther up the Narrows I missed one brook trout and landed two others— the best a 4-pounder, according to Cliff—on a Parachute Wulff. The guides here have handled so many of these fish that they can guess their weights to within an ounce or two and, unlike obsequious guides I've met elsewhere, they refuse to overestimate in order to flatter the clients.

When the floatplane dropped us at Fifth Rapids the next day, the sky was low and gray, and by the time we got on the water the wind was howling. Our guide, Anthony, eased the canoe through a puzzle of boulders and fast currents to a gravelly bar that let us wade to within casting distance of several good pools. Fifth can be rotten with brook trout in midsummer, but this time we found a handful of fish ghosting through like migrating salmon. I was fishing a pair of weighted nymphs on a tight line and having a hell of a time controlling my drift in the wind, but even then, I managed a 3-, a 4-, and a 5-pounder, in that order, over the next few hours. Later, with the canoe nosed into a side channel known as Little Fifth, I hung a 6-pound male resplendent in spawning colors with a humpback and a round, hard gut. These fish had been hard to locate during the season, but they'd apparently been somewhere getting fat on something.

We spent that night at the outpost cabin with another guide and two other sports. After dinner—which at Fifth is always a pot of spaghetti with homemade marinara sauce—I lay in my bunk trying to read a mystery novel over the din of a violent game of cribbage in the kitchen. Every cabin I've been in between Wisconsin and the Arctic Circle has contained a cribbage board and a dog-eared deck of cards, but I refuse to learn the game as a matter of principle.

Before we turned in, Anthony locked the cabin door. That seemed like a pointless precaution there in the middle of nowhere, but he said it was because the bears here have learned that if they push on the door repeatedly they can jiggle the latch open and stroll into the kitchen for a midnight snack. "It sounds like someone's knockin'," Anthony said.

The next day we worked our boat down through Forth and Third Rapids—or as Anthony would say, "Fort" and "Turd"—and in both places we found a few fish scattered through the slower glides. They weren't rising to the few brown caddis flies that were fluttering over the current, but you could sometimes convince one of them to look at a small, soft-hackled wet fly dropped behind an Elk Hair Caddis.

I hooked a 7-pound buck that picked up my dropper in the long glide at the bottom of Forth. The take was so unobtrusive that the only indication of it was when the dry fly sank in a defeated way, as if it had gotten waterlogged. The fish bulldogged in place when I tightened up, then got its bearings and ran downstream into a wide riffle, peeling off line and backing. I followed until I was stopped by deep water while the fish parked out in the fast current, refusing to move. It was a standoff and I had no choice but to try to pump him back, right up against what I judged to be the breaking strength of my tackle. The last few yards were the hardest, and even after Anthony had the fish in the net I couldn't shake the mental image of the size 16 hook bending open or breaking off and couldn't believe that neither calamity had happened. I inhaled deeply in relief and realized it was the first breath I'd taken in some time.

Bob waded over to look at the fish and said, "That's a nice one. I thought you guys were just fuckin' around."

Back at the lodge, Tom, Colin, and Jeremy trooped off every morning like people going to work, which they were. Shooting a fishing movie isn't really fishing any more than filming a love story is

the same as falling in love. You do have to find fish and catch a few
(at which point a normal fisherman would declare success and head
back to camp for a drink) but you also have to deal with constantly
changing locations, light, weather, pitching boats, uncooperative
fish, and awkward camera angles, and record the proceedings on
microphones that aren't hissing in the wild or muffled by clothing, all
without dropping any irreplaceable electronics in the water.

The real artistry comes in the editing. You're aiming for a
documentary sensibility, but the finished product can just as easily
come off as a rock video with fish or a cheesy reality show that's
clumsily scripted and poorly acted by amateurs. I know this only
because I've appeared in a couple of these films: something I agreed
to not because I longed to see my face on the silver screen, but
because I've reached that point in every writer's career when he has
to address the question, "Jeez, is *he* still around?"

At Rick's Surprise, Bob and Ned fished the creek for brook trout
while Emile and I worked the inlet for pike and lake trout. My friend
Robin, the lodge owner, had asked me to check out a few spots for
these two species that will never take top billing away from the big
brook trout, but that can sometimes be used to salvage what would
otherwise be a desperately slow day.

It looked like an ideal spot. I imagined that lake trout would be
nosed into the fan of current where the creek entered the lake, while
northern pike would be lurking at the edges of the moving water and
scattered on out into the boulder-strewn little bay. I'd pictured this so
vividly that at first I was surprised that I wasn't getting a strike on every
cast. I fished out to the end of my casting range and then paid extra
slack line into the current to get my fly even farther out. I became
obsessed with the idea that all the big, hungry fish were just a little
farther out than I could reach. Then, when I finally did get a take, I
muffed it. There was a yank on the line, a tweak as the hook caught

for a split second and then came loose, and a boil containing the flash of a long orange flank. Emile, who'd been standing behind my left shoulder so quietly that I'd forgotten he was there, said, "That was a big brook trout," at the exact instant I came to the same realization.

Later, casting to the right of the inlet, I caught a pair of three-foot-long pike and then went into an hour-long slump. We took a break and talked about Emile's studies at the university and the hard but wholesome life of a guide, and wondered if we really have any grasp at all on what happens in the rudimentary brains of fish or just make stuff up to pass the time.

After we'd rested the inlet I swung it again with the biggest, gaudiest deer hair bug I had, hoping to catch a big pike, and instead got a 6-pound brook trout that looked incongruous with that huge, parti-colored pike fly hanging from his jaw. Maybe it was the same one I'd missed earlier.

The eponymous surprise here for Rick—Robin's brother—was that the creek held only small fish until he got down to the last few long, deep plunge pools above the lake and landed a couple of bruisers. The surprise this time was that the big boys were still staged in the lake, waiting for whatever mysterious signal it might be that would send them squirting up the ankle-deep riffle into the creek.

After dinner at the lodge that night, Jeremy got on his laptop to go over some footage he'd shot and I couldn't resist looking over his shoulder. It was wonderful stuff: one fat brook trout after another rolling to the surface to take gurgler-style flies in clear water, shot at high speed and then slowed down almost imperceptibly to produce a kind of dreamlike effect. Unedited as it was, this sequence compressed a day's worth of action into a fast-paced five minutes, leaving the impression of an orgy of nonstop fish catching and shortchanging the usual blank space between hookups that some call "downtime" but others recognize as the soul of the sport.

Marco Four is one of a set of short rapids named after the bush pilot who was at the camp the first few times I fished there and whom all of us who remember him still refer to as "a piece of work." There were only two good runs to fish here. Bob and Cliff took the first riffly glide, where Bob immediately started hooking brook trout—nice ones, too—while I waded downstream to what I thought looked like the better of the two spots: a deep, boulder-strewn pool with a good current along its far bank and a wide, rocky tail-out.

But half an hour later I'd only managed to skate up one small brook trout along the far bank before the biggest northern pike I'd ever seen in Labrador bit off my fly so cleanly I didn't even feel a tug. As I reeled in to tie on a fresh fly, I noticed movement in the pool and looked down into the face of a large river otter, treading water and glaring at me disdainfully. That's when the light went on. It seemed clear that these two predators had run all the brook trout out of this lovely pool and into the riffle above, where Bob continued to land them with unhurried efficiency. You try not to notice, but my best guess was that he was on about his fifteenth fish by then. Meanwhile, the otter and I silently confronted each other at a range of only a few yards, but across a vast evolutionary gulf: two fishing mammals, neither of us all that glad to see the other.

On the last afternoon in camp I was back at the cabin early. I built a fire in the stove with exaggerated care, delaminating cardboard and shaving spruce kindling with a pocketknife before piling on a few split rounds and then fine-tuning the draft. Then I hung my waders to dry and walked over to the lodge in the rain for a cup of coffee from one of the pots that are perpetually simmering on the woodstove.

I said hello to Kev and Francis—the camp manager and his wife—and nodded at Robin, who was talking on the satellite phone. I gathered that the weather that had grounded us here also had the de Havilland Otter that was scheduled to fly us out tomorrow backed up by a day, so Robin was arranging for a second Otter out of Schefferville, Quebec. It was a glimpse into the day-to-day sausage making that goes on behind the scenes of any fish camp.

The cabin was already too warm by the time I got back, so I cracked a window and took my coffee out on the porch to listen to the rain sizzling on the lake. Judging from the boats tied up at the dock, some fishermen were still out, while a few others had also come in early and I could see smoke rising from the chimneys of their cabins. This camp usually bustles with activity, but at that moment it looked like a small, sleepy village settling in for the winter.

It was about then that Tom ambled up the boardwalk from the dock, dripping rainwater from the brim of his hat and grinning. They'd had the same kind of day as the rest of us: motoring from one normally dependable spot to another, either not finding fish at all or finding them only as hapless singles that seemed lost. The guides blamed it on this weird year that had thrown everything off kilter and they may have wondered privately if this was an anomaly or a preview of the new normal.

But then, on a hunch, their young guide, Brady, ran them out to a spot no one had ever thought to fish before—a nondescript little bay fed by an equally unimpressive creek—and found it to be boiling with lake trout. There they had easily boated twenty-five fish weighing up to 18 pounds, and Jeremy got it all on film, filling out their shooting schedule in the last hour of their last day.

At the lodge that evening, Brady shyly accepted the congratulations of his clients and, more important, the approval of the older guides. He was new that year, an earnest and steady kid who didn't look quite old enough to shave. Robin told me he was a fine guide already and he'd be among the best if he stuck with it, but added that it's a lot to ask of these young guys to return to guiding every year when they can sign on at the iron mine in Wabush and, after a few years' apprenticeship, pull down a six-figure salary. A good living versus the life you want to live—it's a hard choice we all make and then try not to regret—but whatever he decides to do, there'll now be a meat bucket here known as Brady's Cove.

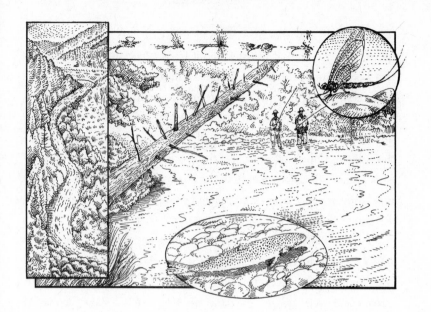

8

OLD WATER

The first time I fished this river, a friend and I stayed at the Little Maud Campground, next to a snowmelt tributary that was too small to hold fish but cold enough to refrigerate our beer. Gerald Ford was president, having succeeded to the office after Richard Nixon resigned in disgrace over the Watergate scandal. At least everyone understood it was a disgrace except Nixon himself, who, when he boarded Marine One for the last time, flashed that weirdly inappropriate double V for victory sign. Victory over what? Like other crooked politicians before and since, the son of a bitch thought he could bluff his way through anything.

You could say the river was an infant fishery then, since the bottom-draw dam that transformed it from a freestone to a tailwater had been completed only a decade earlier. Releases from the dam produced more uniform water temperatures and a longer growing season in the river below, which led to more biomass, but less diversity—the classic tailwater profile. A biologist once told me that the full transition can take a century or more to complete as organisms jostle to find their niches in the changing environment, but that, in a larger sense, it's never complete because it's in the nature of rivers always to have unfinished business.

So that first trip amounted to picking up a long story in the middle and trying to make sense of it, but then that's always how it is on an unfamiliar river. In fact, it was a perfectly recognizable trout stream and we were recognizable trout fishermen, so we managed to catch some fish. They were mostly rainbows at the time, with the occasional brown, the even more occasional brook trout, and a once-in-a-blue-moon cutthroat. There was a time when any trout in this drainage would have been a Colorado River cutthroat, but whether the ones we sometimes caught there in the late '70s were that subspecies or another that had been dumped in as part of the usual twentieth-century hodgepodge of stocking, I can't say. There are fishermen who can identify the fourteen surviving strains of cutthroat at a glance, but I'm not one of them.

Once a friend and I hiked into the headwaters of this river to catch what we'd been told were pure-strain Colorado River cutthroats from a string of high-elevation beaver ponds. The fish were there, but were they holdouts from the original population, as we wanted to believe, or had they been planted later by well-meaning fisheries managers? You can find these things out, but there are reasons not to. Along the same lines, I once heard a rumor from a musician friend that Jerry Garcia's ashes are in a mandolin case that's handed off from one traveling band to the next so that he's always on tour. If that's not true, I don't want to know about it.

Ernest Schwiebert mentioned this river before the dam was built in his 1955 book, *Matching the Hatch*. (We call it a river now, but in the '50s they called it a creek, which should give you an idea of its size.) There are still plenty of caddis flies, but none of my friends and I can remember seeing the clouds of them that Schwiebert described, although we *have* seen the big mayflies that he called Great Red Quills but that, by the time we came along, had been renamed Slate-winged Drakes. They used to come off toward the end of the Green Drakes and then sputter on into the fall, but by the time we pulled the plug on the Green Drakes because the river had gotten too crowded at the height of the hatch, we hadn't seen a Slate-winged Drake in years. Too bad, because the pattern we used to tie for it was one of the handsomest dry flies I've ever seen, with its blue dun hen wings, dun tail, golden-brown-dyed grizzly hackle, and a maroon-dubbed body with a chartreuse rib. It was a departure from Schwiebert's original pattern only because everyone thinks he has a better idea.

Among the other hatches that have come and gone were some size 14 pale yellow mayflies the locals called Sulphurs to distinguish them from the smaller Pale Morning Duns. One year these bugs were there in good numbers, the trout liked them, and fishermen were left scratching their heads and tying size 14 Light Cahills and Ginger Quills. They were important for a few seasons and then abruptly dwindled to the occasional sighting of a single fly over the water, but I still carry a few of the old patterns in case they make a comeback.

There are also the weird little Seratella mayflies that, on this drainage, are said to have evolved to be flightless, hermaphroditic, and born pregnant. Even the local hotshots are still trying to figure these things out and we don't even mention them to visitors because they think we're joking.

That's where things stood when I invited my friend Mike out to fish the river. We'd met in Labrador and later he showed me around some spring creeks in Wisconsin and in Minnesota, where he now lives. You could say I was returning the favor and not be wrong, although that sounds more transactional than it really was.

By then I'd been fishing here for so long that I'd come to know the river the way you know old friends, that is, as much for who they used to be as for who they are now. So when Mike wrote and asked what flies he would need, I typed up a long list of patterns that had been useful over the previous decades, then realized it was ridiculously long and, after several edits, got it down to a modest selection of mayflies, caddis, and midges. Then I dug through my own flies and put together a selection for him that I'd feel okay about fishing myself. That exercise made me realize I was carrying far more flies than I needed, but I didn't do anything about it.

Mike stayed at my house the night he got in and we drove to the river the next morning. It takes five hours to go from 6,000 feet on the east slope of the Rockies and over the Continental Divide to roughly the same elevation on the west slope. That's a ten-hour round-trip, so you have to stay over, and then once you've stayed over you might as well fish for a few more days to make the trip worthwhile. That's how it's always gone. The river is a little too far away to be able to call it our home water, but it feels like home when we're there.

There are plenty of other places I could have taken Mike— and probably will on subsequent visits—but there was no question this first time. This river is a gem when you hit it right and we feel we know enough to hit it right more often than not. There's also something to be said for casting to trout that are the descendants of fish you caught in the past, even if they don't always measure up to their ancestors. Fishing old water is like talking to an ex-wife: there's always a second, longer conversation in the shadow of the one you're currently having. That deep familiarity is compelling. Thomas McGuane once wrote, "Young fishermen love new rivers the way they love the rest of their lives," but older fishermen, "like sentimental drunks, are interested in what they already know."

The group of us who fish here together has changed over time, with people dropping out and joining up at about the same rate, but gradually enough that it still somehow seems like the same old gang. Without really trying, we've always kept it hovering right around the manageable number of four fishermen; more than a partnership, but far short of a full board of directors.

We used to camp to save money and, not incidentally, because we enjoyed the simple but time-consuming chores of pitching tents, getting firewood together, and cooking plain meals on a camp kitchen. Not to mention the oddly memorable moments that come up while camping, like the time a cottonwood tree blew over in a windstorm, missing my parked pickup by inches, or the night I had trouble getting the campfire lit and thought, *People start fires by accident every day; why can't I do it on purpose?*

We soon moved from Little Maud to a friend's land along the river, where we had a better campsite right on the water in an open stand of narrow-leaf cottonwoods. When that eventually fell through for the usual complicated reasons, we rented motel rooms in town, where there's no need to split kindling or heat river water to wash dishes so we sometimes end up watching TV. We're all solvent enough now that we can rent rooms without worrying about the cost, but we've also gotten busier and our time is no longer entirely our own, so it's harder than it used to be to throw a trip together at the last minute.

Now and then there have been guests, like the venerable bamboo rod maker from back east whose long, straight, elegant casts were lovely to watch but useless in this pocket of water, so we had to give him a refresher course in high-sticking and mending—presuming to teach the old master new tricks.

There was an investment banker who was a nice enough guy and a decent fisherman, but he wouldn't stop talking about money and kept trying to organize things that didn't need organizing. He wasn't invited back.

There was the magazine editor, also from back east, who fit in so seamlessly that he now has a standing invitation that, for reasons of his own, he's never cashed in.

I assumed that Mike would also fit right in and he did. There were four of us on this trip and after just a few hours it was as if he'd always been there, not that it was much of an accomplishment. Few fishermen are so unusual that our quirks aren't universal, right down to the retelling of the same old stories that would be pointless if they weren't the landmarks of shared memory.

There was supposed to be fifth guy this time—one of the regulars—but he begged off. He'd recently gone to Mongolia to fish for taimen and had come down with a case of what he called "Genghis Khan's revenge," so he stayed home to recuperate ahead of an upcoming elk hunt. When I saw him a few weeks later, he said he was fine, but he looked depleted, as if he'd left some essential part of himself steaming in the morning chill on a riverbank in East Asia. But as sick as he'd been, he'd dragged himself out of his tent long enough to catch a 40-pound taimen and was already planning a return trip.

The fishing that week wasn't as good as I've ever seen it or as slow as it sometimes is. The fishing was fine, and since this is an excellent dry fly river at a good time of year, it was better than most.

Three- and four-part multiple hatches came off and the trout grazed through them as casually as guests at a cocktail party cruising the hors d'oeuvres. It was also about what I'd told Mike to expect, which was a relief because it made me look like I knew what I was talking about.

I'd been unreasonably worried about that. You know how you can be perfectly happy with your own cooking, only to fret about it when you invite someone over for dinner? Maybe the fried chicken will be scorched, the cornbread will be dry, the mashed potatoes will be lumpy, and your polite guest says, "Oh no, it's fine; just like Mom used to make."

Showing a friend around a favorite river is like that. Rivers have their unpredictable moods, and seasons run together in your mind, so you wonder if your supposedly current reports are actually just an anthology of forty-year-old memories. If things go south, your friend will say, "Hey, it's fishing, I get it," but that will only make you feel worse. We've all seen sentiment outlast reality. There's a little once-secret mountain creek near my home that's not a secret anymore and so isn't what it used to be. Still, so many of us locals want to be cremated and scattered there that eventually the place will look like an ashtray.

But the fishing was fine, as I said. We had bright, cool October weather and the canyon was as handsome as ever with its rust-colored cliffs and dense green pine and spruce woods, while down along the river the willows, dogwoods, sumacs, and bigtooth maples were easing into their fall colors. There were scattered mackerel clouds in the blue sky, suggesting a change in the weather, and in fact one of the first big winterlike storms was due to reach us from the Pacific Northwest later in the week. The forecast called for feet of snow and temperatures cold enough to freeze fly line in the guides, so we'd have to think about sneaking out ahead of it. There are two alpine passes between here and home—one reaching to over 11,000 feet—and we all have horror stories of grinding over these mountains in four-wheel drive, dodging insane flatlanders in Humvees and jackknifed eighteen-wheelers. But for the moment we had chilly mornings and Indian summer afternoons with trout rising like clockwork. And by this late in the year we'd all long since worked out the off-season kinks and were fishing well.

By October the summer fishermen had begun to thin out and we got most of our favorite spots by simply showing up an hour before anyone else, thereby making the river seem less crowded than it really was. I don't know if Mike found that selection of flies I'd given him useful or not. He'd brought his own fly boxes from home and he's a good fisherman who grew up in Montana, so none of this would have been new to him. I felt that my years here should have given me the kind of inside track I could pass along like a savvy old guide, but there was really nothing an observant fisherman couldn't suss out for himself in half a day, including the presence of the odd Green Drake. These big mayflies fade as a predictable hatch by mid-September, but they continue to dribble off in sparse numbers through October, and since the fish are used to seeing them, they recognize them instantly. The rule of thumb is that if you see even one or two of these big flies on or over the water—and they're hard to miss—it's worth switching to a Drake pattern. But, as I said, Mike would have already known that.

But the more common solution was to go smaller instead of larger—something else Mike would have known. One day I located a pod of rising trout that were obviously feeding on size 18 Olive mayflies, but they wouldn't even look at the same sized Sprout emerger or quill-bodied parachute. So I tried a size 22 on a dropper, then switched to a 24 and finally to a size 26, the smallest dry fly I'm able to tie, and even then only on a good day. There was almost nothing to it: just a thread body, infinitesimal plastic wings, and two wispy turns of the smallest possible dun hackle plucked with tweezers from the base of the cock's comb on a rooster neck. But it worked and I managed to land five or six nice trout before the commotion put down the rest of the pod.

This is an old trick on these selective tailwaters. Some claim there's an invisible masking hatch that only the youngest, sharpest eyes can see, while others who imagine themselves matching wits with a brain smaller than a black-eyed pea think it has to do with the trout's mysterious predatory triggers. My theory is that the fish assume that anything that small couldn't possibly be fake.

We did catch a few rainbows—always an event now because the remaining 'bows here tend to be on the larger side and they're really handsome—but this is now predominantly a brown trout river. The fish aren't exactly stunted, but the thinking is that they'd be bigger if there were fewer of them, so there is now a slot limit of two browns no longer than 14 inches on this otherwise catch-and-release water, hoping fishermen will thin them out by eating them. But most fishermen don't, including us. Back when we still camped on the water, we'd now and then have a fresh brown trout dinner, but there's no way to fry them in the motel room, so we release the trout and live on burgers and fries, as fishermen do.

The fishing was good enough that Mike and I stayed on an extra day after our two partners left, but we still made it back over the mountains ahead of the storm. The plan was to fish for two more days in the shelter of the east slope while it snowed like all get-out on the west side. It would be cold, but the hometown tailwater would be good and the big freestone an hour's drive north might also fish okay, although we'd probably be reduced to nymphs and split shot. Fishing is always a calculation, and it gets thornier as the season begins to wind down.

By the time we'd talked out our plans, we were coming down

off the second pass on a dry road surrounded by snow-dusted peaks. In the temporary silence Mike was watching the scenery and I was thinking about rivers: how they're as mortal as we are, but in geologic time, so that in our limited way of seeing things, they seem to last forever, perpetually recycling the world's water from snowpack to oceans and back again—the same water we've always had or ever *will* have.

9

GUIDES

I thought guiding was a glamorous profession, until I tried it. I had imagined it as fishing for a living, which sounded too good to be true and was. In fact, as a guide you're *not* fishing—the tip-off is that you're carrying a net, but no rod—you're helping other people fish, some of whom need more guidance than you, or anyone, could possibly provide. My failures don't make for good stories because they were more pitiful than spectacular and didn't resolve into lessons learned in time for that wisdom to be useful to me or my clients. Simply put, I was no damned good at guiding and didn't last long, but in my defense, I was young, and although I'd done a fair amount of fly-fishing and wasn't bad at it, I'd never actually been guided and had no idea how it was done.

I later learned that it's done as many different ways as there are guides, although you may notice some regional similarities. When I first fished in Labrador more than thirty years ago, I was lucky enough to go out with some old-school Canadian brook trout guides. As this laconic bunch saw it, their job consisted of putting you in a canoe, taking you to the right spot, and netting your fish if you caught any, but there was no instruction or entertaining banter and the sometimes-insurmountable distance between getting there and landing a brook trout was entirely up to you. I mean, you're the fisherman, right?

Sometimes you could pry out an opinion by asking, "What do you think here, dry fly or streamer?" But even then they were likely to shrug and say, "Your choice" or "Either could work." Like cabdrivers, they'd take you where you were supposed to go, but it wasn't in their job description to help out with what you were supposed to do once you got there. Some sports from the United States who'd grown used to the more obsequious American style of guiding felt neglected. They didn't appreciate that their guide was paying them the compliment of assuming they knew what they were doing.

I actually preferred a silent Canadian leaning on his long-handled landing net to the in-your-face style of guiding that was sweeping the West at the time. I don't qualify as an expert fisherman and I've always been happy to listen to advice, but I've never felt the need to have a guide select my fly, tie it on for me, tell me where and how to cast it, and then yell "SET!" in my ear when I got a take.

But having failed as a guide myself, I understand that this comes from frustration. You quickly tire of inaccurate casts, motorboat dry fly drifts, granny knots that come loose at the first tug, and clients who sleepwalk through solid takes, so SET! for Christ's sake!

The most adamant about tying your flies on for you are the steelhead and Atlantic salmon guides, and it makes sense. In these depleted times you can cast for days or even weeks before you hook one of these anadromous fish and there's plenty that can go wrong when you do—ranging from operator error to acts of God—so at the very least, you want a solid knot.

I fished an Atlantic salmon river in Labrador with a guide who sort of let me choose my own fly (he winced at my first choice, grimaced at my second, and allowed himself just the hint of a smile and a single nod of the head at my third) but when I went to tie it on he said, "Here, let me," in a tone of voice that didn't leave room for discussion.

We were fishing skaters that required a riffling hitch, a knot that puts the leader at a more or less right angle to the hook shank— to the left or the right depending on the direction of the current. To true believers, this is the only way to make a skated fly pull the proper serpentine wake on the surface that's supposed to produce a take. The salmon I hooked was less than a mile from the ocean, still had sea lice, and repeatedly jumped as high as my head—but the knot held.

I was on a salmon river in New Brunswick once with a Mi'kmaq Indian guide named Helen, who I thought might let me tie on my own fly. She suggested a pattern—an Allie's Shrimp—and watched as I tied it to my leader with a Turle knot. Then she took it, examined the knot carefully from every angle, bit it off, and retied it with a Turle knot of her own that, I thought, looked exactly like mine. I caught two salmon that day and, again, the knot held.

I've seen this go wrong only once. My friend Vince and I were fishing a steelhead river in the Pacific Northwest with a guide who, as usual, insisted on tying our flies on for us. But then Vince hooked an enormous steelhead that jumped once in a big silver arc and ran back toward the ocean, peeling off half his backing before the rod went limp. When he reeled in, the fly was gone and there was the pigtail at the tip of the leader that meant the knot hadn't broken, it had pulled loose.

I learned all that later. All I saw when I came around the bend from upstream was our guide sitting on a log with his shoulders slumped and his face in his hands as if he were contemplating suicide, while Vince patted him on the back and said, "It's okay, man. It could have happened to anyone."

Years ago, I went out on a river in Colorado with a guide who had adopted the full drill sergeant persona. That would be the Hollywood version of a drill sergeant, since he'd never actually served in the military. He barked orders and criticized everything from my fly choices, to my casting, my wading, my rod, my leader, and the knots I tied. "You call that an improved clinch?" he'd shout. At least he stopped short of calling me "Maggot."

But he knew his stuff. All day long he led my partner and me unerringly from one pod of rising trout to the next like a pointer sniffing out coveys of quail; he could decode masking hatches at a glance, tell by the rise forms whether a trout was taking dry flies or floating nymphs, and had an eye for big, solitary bank sippers that I'd have walked right past. He was an old friend of the guy I was fishing with and had offered to take us out on his day off. He wouldn't hear of being paid and I was glad of that, so I didn't have to wonder if a tip commensurate with his skill would be misinterpreted as encouragement for being a dick.

I was a little apprehensive years later in Wisconsin when I went out with a smallmouth bass guide who was nicknamed "Sarge," but it was only because his last name was Sergeant and he turned out to be as mellow and helpful as they come; a real pleasure to spend time with.

Guides who work at remote lodges in places like Labrador, Alaska, or the Northwest Territories aren't better or tougher than those who go home to sleep in their own beds every night, but there's a noticeable difference in their level of commitment. Signing on for a season at a wilderness lodge is like joining the French Foreign Legion. You'll be spending your time far from home, out in the weather by day and sleeping rough at night. (The hooches where the guides stay aren't as posh as the guest cabins, to put it mildly.) The job description says "fishing guide," but they'll also be expected to do whatever else needs doing: cutting, splitting, and stacking firewood, cleaning out the boats, fixing outboard motors, hauling garbage, repairing docks, patching leaky cabin roofs, and so on. (Some guides have learned to keep quiet about whatever carpentry or plumbing skills they might have, for fear of extra work.) In Alaska they'll probably also end up carrying a firearm in case of run-ins with bears, but they don't get extra combat pay and are usually expected to supply their own weapons and ammunition. And they'll probably be expected to arrive a week early to open the camp and then stay late to get the place buttoned up for winter.

The isolated society of a fishing lodge has aspects of both a family and a job, complete with a pecking order and all the comforts and heartaches that come with both. Although the whole enterprise amounts to a service economy that depends on the clients, the fishermen themselves just come and go like the weather, only on a more predictable schedule.

Most of the guides at wilderness camps are young and energetic. They run boats, drop and pull anchors, tie on flies, net fish, untangle leaders, and troubleshoot their clients in countless other ways. At the end of a day they'll often do a few chores and then sit up late around an open fire telling stories about boat wrecks, floatplane crashes, and bear attacks until the fishermen get sleepy and go to bed. Then they'll stay up even later talking about the idiot clients they've guided. Occasionally some alcohol is consumed.

In the morning, when we tourists blunder over to the lodge for coffee at what would be the crack of dawn if the midnight sun would ever set, they're already up and bustling around, fresh as daisies.

Sometimes the head guide at one of these places will be an old-timer in his forties or even fifties and, every once in a while, there'll be an older, more seasoned rank-and-file guide in camp who functions—usually unofficially—as an advisor to the younger guys. I met a guide like that on the Aniak River in Alaska recently. His name was Ron and he was an ex-Marine, although, like so many of the breed I've known, there was no "ex" about it and his off-season guide service back home was called "Semper Fly." If any guide could have pulled off the drill sergeant routine, it was him, but he was just the opposite—probably because he had nothing whatsoever to prove—and he had those big Alaskan rainbows wired. He was also the only one in camp who wore his big-bore sidearm without a touch of swagger, as if it were no more lethal than a wallet.

I'm told that when these guys finally come home after a season at a fish camp, there's a period of decompression while they reacquaint themselves with things like traffic, bright lights, crowds, noise, television, and whatever friends and family they'd left behind. I've known guides who drank and smoked during the season and then abruptly quit both habits when they boarded their flight home, without any outward signs of withdrawal. I've also seen guides fresh from the bush duck their heads when they enter a room as if, after months spent under an open sky, the ceiling—any ceiling—is too low.

Guides sometimes exhibit seasonal changes that mimic those you'll see in the fishery itself. Some of the younger ones who haven't yet learned to pace themselves will hit the ground running in the spring. Drunk on youth and enthusiasm, they'll take on extra chores and work their soft, middle-aged clients like rented mules, only to become burnt-out zombies by fall. More experienced guides will set a gait they can maintain, but that's not a guarantee that they won't get what's sometimes known as the Red Ass. Too many leaky boats and broken-down outboards, too many spats with colleagues and management, too many extra chores, too many clients who can't or won't listen and then skimp on their tip because they didn't catch enough fish, too much time to balance a season's wages against a winter's rent, and you can begin to wonder if coming here was the right choice after all.

Other times it's no more specific than the guiding equivalent of the seven-year itch in a marriage, so that after months of nothing but good home cooking, all you want is a Big Mac and fries. Or occasionally it's the opposite. I once fished with a guide in Canada who, by late in the season, had gone native and wasn't happy about the prospect of leaving the backcountry for "civilization," a word he pronounced as if it were a terminal disease.

I think the most useful quality a guide can have is adaptability—both to the sometimes-bizarre range of clients he'll get as well as to the constantly changing weather and water conditions that can make such a big difference in the fishing. The Chinese once recognized seventy-two seasons every year, each lasting only a few days, and those who make their livelihoods on rivers begin to see their world the same way: always familiar, but fluid enough to look a little bit different every morning. Another guide I know who's also an ex-Marine once told me his motto for guiding is the same as it was in the service: "Semper Gumby," or always flexible.

Some guides, especially the younger ones, run the same program on all their clients, usually geared to the lowest common denominator. But the best of them develop the ability to size up their fishermen—often at a glance—and tailor the day to who they are and the sometimes vast difference between what they want and expect and what they're capable of. These are the guys who eventually end up with a waiting list of repeat customers and who seldom fish with people they don't already know. That describes an old friend of mine. Clients would call the shop where he worked and ask to book a trip with Chris, but if he wasn't available and another guide was offered, they'd say "Nah, we'll just come back later."

Here's a tip: don't play poker with someone who can read people that easily. If you have a tell—and most of us do—they'll have it down in three hands and they'll take you to the cleaners.

I've fished with a lot of guides in the forty years since I gave up guiding myself. A precious handful of them were absolute masters at it: so subtly and effortlessly good that sometimes it was only in hindsight that it dawned on me just how good they were, while at the time it seemed like the day was going especially smoothly and I was really on my game. There's being so good you make guiding look easy, and then there's being so good your fisherman doesn't even notice he's being guided.

Among the others, most were anywhere from competent but unmemorable, to good, to exceptional, and we usually caught fish if catching fish was in the cards. (No guide, however talented, can make the fish bite if the fish aren't biting.) Now and then a guide would be good in every way that counts, but have an annoying quirk.

A friend and I once had a guide in Alberta we took to calling Laughing Jack because he laughed at everything, whether it was funny or not. If you said the river was beautiful, he'd laugh. If you asked what fly to tie on, he'd laugh. He'd have laughed if you told him your mother just died. It was a nervous tic that probably had to do with insecurity, but it got on our nerves.

There are guides who overinstruct, and those who spend the day bragging about what good guides they are, as if you weren't right there to see just how good they are, which often isn't very good at all.

There are all too many who'll watch you like a hawk until you get a take, and then yell "SET! SET! SET!" in an apparent panic. On the off chance that they don't startle you into missing the fish and you actually manage to hook up, they'll say, "*There* you go" as if you couldn't possibly have caught that fish without their help. It makes for a long day, during which I wish for a taciturn Newfie who doesn't say a word until your brook trout is in the net, at which point he might venture, "Four and a quarter pounds, ey?"

That's why I've always preferred silent guides to those who talked too much and said too little, filling the stillness of a river with pointless noise like a radio left playing in an empty room.

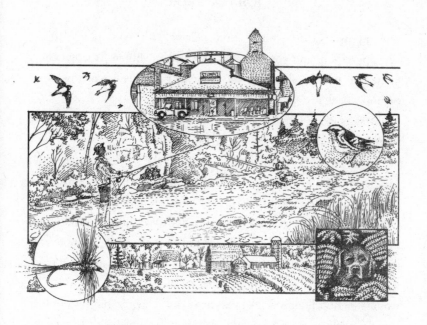

10

THE VIEW FROM STUMPY'S

I've flown into the Minneapolis–St. Paul airport often enough now that everything is familiar, so, like a local coming home, I amble down to baggage claim to retrieve my duffel without bothering to read the signs. The carousel for the Denver flight is opposite the Caribou Coffee kiosk, but I ignore the temptation, knowing we'll stop for a cup on our way out of town.

Outside I look for Mike Dvorak leaning against his SUV while his black Lab, Moose, rubbernecks out the window. When Moose sees me his head begins to bobble from side to side in response to the recoil of his wagging tail. Moose likes everyone, but I think he sees me as a favorite uncle he associates with days spent outside, lax supervision, and generous handouts at lunchtime. In any case, I know that when I slide into the passenger seat he'll reach up from behind to lick my ear and knock my hat off.

Mike is more subdued: a quick, manly hug and then we're out of there.

The familiarity continues to sink in on the drive south into the Minnesota Driftless country, partly from fresh memories of previous trips, but also because I grew up not far from here in the 1950s and early '60s and imprinted on the time and place like a duckling on its mother. Once, Mike even drove me out to see my old house. It looked better than when I lived there—freshly painted and re-roofed, with new doors and windows and the lawn recently mowed. The whole neighborhood was like that now, still recognizable, except that the sidewalks were flat where I remember them being heaved by tree roots and the lake across the road where I spent so much time had lawns running right down to the water, where I remembered a no-man's-land of brush and cattails. The whole place now seemed light on ramshackle sheds, burn barrels, sagging fences, and weed-grown lots laced with aimless footpaths worn by aimless kids and I wondered if the feral adolescence I spent here would still be possible.

We parked in front of the house for a few minutes while I waited to relapse into undiagnosed homesickness at the sight of the place, but it didn't happen. I was happy enough when I lived there—growing pains notwithstanding—but the early 1960s were as bland and monotonous as the '50s had been (at least in Minnesota) and by the age of fourteen I'd already begun to plan my escape. So instead of getting nostalgic, I was just impatient to go fishing—as much right then as I was in 1960.

That evening we pulled into Rushford—a town of 1,700 souls with its grain elevator dominating the two-story skyline like a cathedral at the heart of a city—and checked into the same motel we'd stayed in the year before. It's the cheaper of the two in town and they allow dogs. In the morning we walked a block to Stumpy's Café for breakfast and then stopped at Pam's Corner Convenience and Off-Sale Liquor to buy my nonresident fishing license before pulling out of town on the way to our first creek. Elapsed time since I'd left my driveway for the airport in Denver: a little less than twenty-four hours. Not bad as fishing trips go.

This region of southeast Minnesota consists of green rolling hills and farm country (feed corn, soybeans, alfalfa, dairy, and beef) punctuated by small towns and laced with so many spring-fed creeks, bound eventually for the Mississippi, that you can't drive far in any direction without crossing or paralleling one. Nearby Rush Creek was named for the rushes that grow along its banks, but many of the smaller streams here bear the surnames of current or former landowners because even among unpretentious Minnesotans, it's permissible to think, *My farm; my creek.*

The first settlers found these streams populated with indigenous brook trout way out here on the western edge of their native range. Those fish have now mostly been fished out and replaced by brown trout, under the mistaken assumption that one trout is as good as another. But more recently heritage brook trout have been reintroduced in some places and they still turn up from time to time, most often on the covers of Department of Natural Resources publications.

We started on a stream with a German-sounding name and, as Mike likes to do, we hiked along it until the fisherman's trail petered out before we started casting. The day was cool, humid, and overcast, better weather for Blue-wing Olives than for caddis, we thought, although we'd timed the trip to hit the last of the former, the beginning of the latter, or, if we were lucky, both overlapping.

There were no Olives that day, but there *were* a few caddis flies in the air—nothing you could call a hatch, just a few bugs popping off sporadically. I don't think either of us ever saw a rising trout, but the stream was percolating with activity. Warblers perched on low-hanging branches, now and then darting out over the water to make acrobatic grabs at caddis flies, while swallows patrolled the airspace above for any bugs the warblers missed.

A fisherman naturally assumes that the trout are doing much the same thing underwater, holding in quiet spots in the current and ambushing the odd caddis pupa swimming for the surface. So we tied on floating caddis patterns with weighted dropper flies dangling behind and leapfrogged upstream, prospecting likely looking runs and paying close attention to spots where there were lots of birds.

We caught fish here and there, all brown trout. Most took our droppers a few inches under the surface, but now and then an eager fish would go the full distance to the surface to eat the dry fly. It was hit-and-miss, as fishing often is. Sometimes a spot that looked tantalizing would give up a take or two, while another spot that looked just as good seemed dead. When that happens, one kind of fisherman assumes there were no fish there, while the more realistic among us think they *were* there, but either didn't like our flies or spooked at our first casts.

Sometimes a fish would seemingly come out of nowhere on a random cast as we worked our way from one pool to the next. I'd fished here before, but although it's true that any trout stream seems at least vaguely familiar, it's also true that you can spend years fishing a region before you get a fully informed sense of where the fish will be.

Later on, still thinking about swimming caddis pupae, I tied on a pair of soft-hackled wet flies and swung through some riffles, missing some pulls that seemed halfhearted, but connecting on a handful of others that felt more confident. Maybe there were enough emerging caddis under the surface that the fish were on the lookout for them. Or maybe a swinging fly just triggered their predatory sensibilities without entirely convincing them, like a shoelace wiggled in front of a cat. Or maybe it's just that a traditional wet fly swing covers a pool in methodical concentric stripes so every fish in the run sees it, including the dumb ones. The fact is, you don't always have to know what you're doing in order to catch a few fish, as long as you keep a hook in the water. At the end of this kind of a day's fishing you can feel like you didn't catch that many trout, but then when you think back on it you realize there were more than you thought—more than enough for a meal if you'd kept them, which is the traditional definition of angling success.

You have to love these ordinary days if only because there are so many of them. If all you want from fishing are the rare extreme events—the blizzard hatches and gorging fish—you're doomed to disappointment. Better to take your cue from Moose, who spends his days out searching for things to sniff, pee on, roll in, or chew on. At the end of a mediocre day, a person might say "it was just nice to get out," but a dog would mean that wholeheartedly.

One day we fished a stream that was named after either a Native American tribe of the Great Lakes region or a popular brand of recreational vehicle. It flowed through a typical small valley of well-kept farms surrounded by low hills forested right to their summits with the fresh, spring buds of assorted hardwoods, making a kind of chartreuse haze in the crowns of the trees. (Farms can seem so quiet and pastoral you have to remind yourself how hard these people work.) There were also the odd outcrops of limestone you'll find everywhere along these watercourses, anything from isolated knobs like viewing stones in Japanese gardens to sheer cliff faces, dripping with moss and ferns if they're shaded or looking raw and sand-colored if they're out in the sun.

Limestone is a subtext here. Most important to a fisherman, it slowly dissolves in water and contributes to the rich chemistry of these streams. But you'll also see old buildings made of limestone: a bank building that's now an Italian restaurant, churches, storefronts, an old schoolhouse with a stubby bell tower that's now someone's fashionably rustic home. Now and then, on unpaved county roads, you'll pass old limestone quarries, long since abandoned in favor of concrete and rebar, but still viable.

On the way to the creek we drove past a tall limestone cliff where someone, presumably high school kids, had carved names, dates, and miscellaneous slogans at eye level. Limestone is on the soft side as rock goes, but it's still rock, and I was impressed by the industriousness of these projects that made city taggers with their spray paint seem like slackers. I pictured farm kids working away with chisels and mallets like Egyptians inscribing hieroglyphics, but I suppose battery-operated power tools are more likely.

At the fence stile that marked the state fishing easement on the creek, we spotted two guys working their way downstream (the only other fishermen we saw that week), so we went in the opposite direction. Minnesota's trout stream easement program is extensive enough that you could begin to think you can fish anywhere—and based on the no-nonsense KEEP OUT signs you see from time to time, some do think that—but there's still more than enough public water to go around. So much that you can often arrange to have a whole creek to yourself—or in this case half a creek, which can go on for miles.

This easement system works as well as it does because it's so unambiguous. At the top end of a sliding scale based on stream quality, the Department of Natural Resources will pay as much as $12 per linear foot for a fishing easement. At that rate, a mile of good trout stream will net a farmer $63,360; two miles will go for twice that much and so on. No vague tax breaks or credits, but real cash money in the bank.

Easements are supposed to be marked by 5x7-inch tan-colored signs that are so unobtrusive they're easy to miss and sometimes aren't there at all. You'll have the map booklet published by the DNR, probably backed up by a more detailed gazetteer, but what you're looking for are the fence stiles that keep fishermen from stretching barbed wire and popping staples as they crawl over or through.

You can find a fly shop in this region if you need one, but they're not in every town, let alone on every corner, and you won't see the crowds of tourist fishermen here that haunt places like West Yellowstone, Montana, or Island Park, Idaho. There just don't seem to be that many fishermen around, probably because the fishing is known to be good, but not fabulous in the grand scheme of destination angling, and it's possible that southern Minnesota farm country isn't glamorous enough for some traveling sports. Consequently, the place seems delightfully sleepy and some people who've fished here say it's like fishing used to be.

The day was cool, calm, and cloudy, threatening rain without ever actually raining. We caught fish right along in widely spaced fits and starts, as we had the day before, but there were spells when the fishing was slow enough that I got interested in the birds. I thought I could pick out barn and bank swallows in the air, but mostly they were just fast-moving black silhouettes against a gray sky. Down along the stream I saw Audubon's and yellow warblers, yellowthroats, and Blackburnian warblers. There were others, but as an amateur bird-watcher who was, after all, busy fishing, I had to write them off as head-scratchers.

There were birds everywhere. It was the first full week in May and this region is smack in the middle of the Mississippi flyway, one of four migratory routes that reach across North American like rivers flowing north in the spring and south in the fall. By one estimate, 326 different species regularly use this route and, even in these environmentally benighted times, there are so many individual birds that if they all flew over at once they'd blacken the sky.

On days when the fishing isn't fast and furious, all these birds can be as unwanted a distraction as daydreaming. Once I glanced up at a pretty little bird at the exact moment a trout decided to eat my fly. I somehow managed to hook the fish anyway, but the weight of it surprised me as much as the strike itself had and before I could collect myself, it got in a snag and broke me off. I'd been catching 8- to 10-inch browns and this one was probably more like a 14- or 15-incher, but I never actually saw it. Bigger trout do turn up here, so who knows? When I glanced back at the twig where I thought I'd seen a Townsend's warbler, the bird was gone, too.

Things went on in that vein. The days were anywhere from comfortably cool to chilly; partly cloudy to drizzly to one day of frog-strangling rain that kept us off the water. The caddis flies acted like they were ready to hatch, but were waiting for the weather to clear. In the meantime they'd send up advance scouts, most of which were picked off by trout and birds. It was the kind of fishing that keeps you moving, thinking, and picking apart runs with methodical casts. It was so engrossing that time passed unnoticed, and at the end of each day I'd be surprised to feel my stomach growling for supper.

We did find one Blue-wing Olive hatch. It was on a little stream down in the far southeastern corner of the state that has one name in Minnesota and another when it crosses the nearby border into Iowa, nicely camouflaging its headwaters. (And yes, there is trout fishing in Iowa. Who knew?)

When these streams flow out along the valleys, they sometimes devolve into long stretches of unproductive frog water, but the smaller ones like this, tumbling more steeply out of forested hills, come in what seem like endless, unevenly spaced riffles and pools.

The Olives came off almost as sparsely as the caddis had, but in every likely looking pool there were a few trout casually rising. Fish working a thin hatch can be tough. They don't rise regularly, they don't always stay in one place, and they seem to study your fly patterns more critically. After enough refusals, you can begin to think that your fly, which looked so good when you tied it, now seems clunky and obviously fake. It's a thought you fight off because it plays hell with your confidence. You remind yourself that as long as the fly is close to the right size and color, it's usually the accuracy of the cast and the quality of the drift that make the difference. In the end we caught trout at about the same rate that had characterized the trip—more than enough to declare it another workmanlike day of fly-fishing—and ended at a honey hole with more mayflies and bigger trout than we'd seen all day.

It was a one-man spot so we traded off. The place demanded an upstream slack line cast into complicated currents where the creek braided around some boulders, and there was a lot of algae in the water, so on every second or third drift the fly would foul in the stuff. That meant retrieving the fly, peeling off the sticky green goo, rinsing it clean in the water, false casting to dry it and then redressing with floatant. After a while the white wing on my size 20 parachute dry fly was stained a pale olive color, making it even harder to see on the water.

I owe my last trout of the day to Mike. By then the sun was getting low and the water was so chromy that I was no longer even trying to see my fly. I would just watch the spot where I thought it landed and follow it downstream at current speed. When a nice brown trout rose slightly upstream and a foot to the left of where I thought my fly was, I ignored it until Mike said, "There." My Pavlovian response was to set the hook and, sure enough, there was the fish. If you're like me, you're always a little embarrassed when another fisherman has to call your strike—but you'll take the fish anyway.

All this time Moose sat watching from a patch of ferns with his paws crossed thoughtfully in front of him. He probably wasn't tired, but it was the end of the day and he'd run off a lot of his superfluous doggish energy. I've caught Moose observing us like this before. He's been at this his whole life and knows what a day of fishing means to him, but I don't think he's ever worked out exactly what it is that the people are up to. So now and then he'll stop and study us for a while as if he's trying to work out the rules to an unfamiliar game and wearing the same uncomprehending expression I'd wear while watching a cricket match.

That night we met our friend Dan Frasier at the motel. He'd driven over from South Dakota to fish with us the next day and then planned stay on to fish another day while Mike drove me to the airport. Our mutual artist friend Bob White was supposed to join us, too, but he had to cancel at the last minute. Too jammed up with work and family, he said—the two biggest enemies of the deadbeat.

When we moseyed into Stumpy's for breakfast on our last morning, we finally got a nod of acknowledgment from one of the gray-haired regulars at the philosophers' table (every mom-and-pop café has one). If we'd stayed much longer, one of these guys would have finally ventured, "How's the fishin'?" or "Where you boys from?" and the ice would have been broken. But then a distinguishing feature of most fishing trips is that you're there and gone before your presence fully registers, leaving your status as a stranger unsullied. You caught a few trout and spent a few dollars, but otherwise it's like you were never there.

11

WET WADING

If there were no other way to tell, I'd still know it was wet-wading season by looking down at my legs. By July of most years, my winter-white skin is finally tanned from two months of wearing shorts, and there are the inevitable scrapes, and bruises in various stages of healing, plus pale scars from previous seasons that vanish over the winter, only to show up again in negative as the sun develops the pigment in my skin for another year. (My hands are the same story. Apparently, I can't perform the simplest operation without getting nicked by something or skinning a knuckle.)

It goes without saying that I wear shorts for comfort in hot weather, not to show off my legs. A woman I know says that once men get past the age of thirty-five, they should start covering themselves up as a public service.

I came late to wet wading after spending the requisite number of years trying to stay dry in all conditions by habitually wearing waders whenever I went fishing—stiff, heavy rubberized canvas, flimsy latex, suffocating neoprene, and breathable Gore-Tex, more or less in that order over the years. And I still usually do, since fully two-thirds of my fishing is done in cool, chilly, or outright cold weather when there's no sane alternative to trying to stay dry. I suppose my Minnesota upbringing set the stage. Up there you had bitter cold for half the year, swarms of stinging insects the other half, and if you went for a quick swim or just waded bare-legged in the shallows to cool off, you could spend the next half hour removing leeches. As a he-man in training, I never let my squeamishness show, but these slimy parasitic worms secretly turned my stomach. The best method was to sprinkle salt on them and then wait for them to writhe around and spit you out on their own. (Your first impulse was to pull, but if you did that you'd get skin along with the leech.) So it wasn't just Midwestern modesty that made me shy of exposing too much skin.

Like many of the most useful things I know about fishing, I picked up wet wading from guides. These guys were on the water almost daily in season and had long since puzzled out the quickest, easiest, and most comfortable way to do things. No telling how many hot summer days I cooked in full chest waders while the guide pulled the oars dressed comfortably in shorts and sandals before I began to see the light. Also, although I'm still not entirely sure why any of us fly-fish, being one with nature is high on everyone's list, and it's hard to feel at one with nature when you're wearing rubber pants that resemble a hazmat suit.

For that matter, after spending decades in what the tackle industry would like us to think is a gear-heavy sport, you can begin to pine for those childhood days of barefoot fishing with nothing but a cane pole and a can of worms—even if your only actual experience with that came from Norman Rockwell paintings. Whatever the reason, the day comes when you look at your lifelong accumulation of expensive tackle and equipment and wonder, *Does every afternoon of fishing really have to be a full-scale expedition?*

Fly-fishing is famous as an enterprise where more can go wrong than right and usually does, so of course wet wading has its own peculiar pitfalls. More than once I've walked right into the wild rosebushes with their pretty pink flowers and thousands of tiny but sharp thorns that are common around here and then tried to tiptoe back out again without making it worse, which turns out to be impossible. This isn't serious—it's more on the order of being attacked by a litter of week-old kittens—but the hundreds of tiny white scratches still sting and itch.

Once, after wet wading in a warm-water pond casting for carp, I cut across country through some tall grass back to where my pickup was parked without noticing that much of that tall grass was actually stinging nettle. I was sorry for days.

One day when I was working my way around on the bank of a nearby stream to get a good casting angle on a nice-sized brown trout, I found myself standing bare-legged in a large patch of poison ivy that I would have noticed sooner if I hadn't been distracted by that fish. I saved my bacon that time by wading into the stream and scrubbing my legs raw with cold water and handfuls of sand. At least I had the presence of mind to do it downstream, where all my splashing wouldn't spook the trout I was stalking.

Here in northern Colorado, the dependable wet-wading season

lasts roughly from late June to late August, although it expands and contracts at each end from year to year. It works best for me when I'm covering a stretch of small stream on foot, getting in and out of the water constantly, or doing a float where I'm back in the boat high and dry at least half the time. But if I'm on a trip where I'll be wading for hours on end, I still want to be in waders, even if the weather is hot.

On a summer afternoon with temperatures in the 80s or 90s, it can feel blissful to wade bare-legged into water that's in the low 50s, but after you've stood there for an hour you can begin to get pretty cold. This is oddly disconcerting. Your back and shoulders are baking in the sun and your hatband is damp with sweat, while your legs are going numb and your knees are knocking. And of course the trout invariably start biting at the exact moment you decide to get out of the water and stand in the sun to warm up.

Also, conditions can change quickly here in the Rocky Mountains. I do a lot of mid- to late-summer fishing at fairly high elevations, where a sudden squall can drop the temperature by 15 or 20 degrees in minutes—say, from 80 degrees to 60—and if you've been wet wading all afternoon, even just a thin cloud cover and a little breeze can bring on a good chill.

The solution is one I picked up from yet another guide: I carry a cheap pair of wide-legged fleece pants in my day pack. (You want the wide-legged kind so you can pull them on quickly without having to take off your wading boots.) Unlike the special fleece pants designed specifically to be worn by fishermen under waders, you can get these cheaply at any chain discount store you're willing to do business with.

That usually does it. If not, my day pack also holds a wool sweater and a rain slicker, and if things get any more Western than that, I have a fire-starting kit that consists of kiln-dried pine sticks wrapped in newspaper with wooden matches and a striker, all double bagged in plastic. It doesn't seem like it would be that hard to start a fire, but in the kind of conditions that require a fast blaze for warmth, dry matches and kindling can be scarce.

I always carry that little pack if I'll be going more than a few minutes' walk from the truck. Any survival instructor will tell you that if you're very far out for very long you should always have, at a bare minimum, some clothes that are warmer than you think you'll need, a sharp knife, a compass, some high-energy food like granola bars or trail mix, a loud whistle (to attract rescuers), and dry matches.

I don't think I'm being overly cautious here. Several times every year, hapless tourists go for hikes in the mountains on hot summer days dressed in nothing but shorts, T-shirts, and flip-flops, only to get lost or injured and spend several below-freezing nights with no warm clothes, no food, and no way to start a fire unless they're lucky enough to be smokers.

People make all kinds of mistakes, like not telling anyone where they're going and when they expect to be back, or telling them, then changing their minds at the last minute and going somewhere else. And it's easy to hurt yourself hiking in steep, rocky terrain, especially if you get a wild hare and go off-trail. Sprained ankles and broken legs are the most common injuries, but there are plenty of others, including altitude sickness in those not used to high elevations. Also, if you're unconscious or lying down for some other reason, you could be within feet of a trail and go unnoticed by dozens of hikers in an afternoon.

Most eventually turn up on their own or are found by search parties, but now and then search-and-rescue teams bring them out in body bags. We lose one every second or third year on average. It's not that the mountains are so dangerous; it's just that some people are so scared of open country that they won't leave their cars, while others assume everything is here for their convenience and so aren't scared enough.

Every once in a great while someone goes missing and is never found. Search-and-rescue crews look, but not indefinitely. Sometimes friends and family continue the effort for weeks or even months, but eventually it becomes pointless. This doesn't happen often, but it happens just often enough that a convincing way to disappear would be to leave your car at a trailhead and quietly snag a ride to Mexico. Rumor has it that that's been done.

When you live near a national forest, a wilderness area, and a national park that gets four million visitors a year, it's possible to develop a low opinion of tourists. There are inevitably a few real dim bulbs in the mix, but to be fair, this is often less a matter of outright stupidity than it is a lack of regional awareness caused simply by being from somewhere else, so that someone from Seattle always has a raincoat handy, while someone of equal intelligence from Tucson may not even *own* a raincoat.

But outright simple-mindedness isn't unheard-of. A ranger in Rocky Mountain National Park once told me that a strangely common question from tourists is, "When do the deer turn into elk?" (He tells them it happens in October.) So it's not a stretch to think that someone from the flat Midwest might not realize that a trail that gains 3,000 feet in four miles might be a little more of a death march than they imagined or that the shortcut they pictured so clearly on a map might be blocked by an impassable gorge. And now it's dark and they can't find their way back to the trail.

But the complacency that comes with being prepared and familiar with the countryside can also get you into trouble. You get casual; you feel free to cut corners, thinking, *Okay, this bends the rules a little, but I know what I'm doing.*

One August I was fishing a local high-country stream with my two friends Ed and Paul. We'd four-wheeled in about two miles on an old logging road, parked the Jeep, and hiked half a mile back downstream, figuring to slowly fish our way back up to the vehicle in time for a late lunch. It was sunny and warm when we started walking—ideal wet-wading weather—but weather changes quickly here and by the time we got where we wanted to be, charcoal-gray clouds had oozed in against the Continental Divide and it had started to rain.

We dutifully put on our rain jackets and tucked up under the meager shelter of a blue spruce to wait it out, figuring that these mountain thunderstorms seldom last longer than fifteen or twenty minutes. At first this seemed like the normal sprinkle that becomes an outright rain and then a downpour punctuated by lightning and pea-sized hail: the kind of storm that seems apocalyptic, but blows itself out quickly into warm sunlight and a steaming forest. But this turned out to be one of those increasingly common freak storms that back into a high basin and park there all day. (Had this been predicted? I don't know. None of us had bothered to check the weather forecast, because we knew what we were doing.) An hour later it was still raining—harder, if anything—the temperature had dropped into the 40s, the ground was white with hailstones, and the creek had risen eighteen inches and turned shit-brown.

When I started to get chilly I dug into the pack for my fleece pants, but they weren't there. They're supposed to *always* be there, so I looked again, but there aren't that many places for a piece of clothing to hide in a small rucksack. I searched my memory for an image of me taking them out to wash and forgetting to put them back and drew a blank, but by then I may already have been too cold to think straight.

Not long after that, we finally admitted that not only was the fishing blown for the day, but we were all getting pretty damned cold. I assumed the half-mile uphill walk back to the Jeep would warm me up—even in the rain—but it didn't. By the time we got there I was into the first stage of hypothermia, where your tongue feels too thick to speak and you fumble with the car keys through waves of uncontrollable shivering. The natural progression after that would be to disorientation, followed by the false and often fatal sense of warmth and drowsiness that author Mark Spragg called "the thermodynamic lullaby." That's why people dead of exposure are sometimes found half naked: even as their core temperature was dropping, they thought they were too hot.

I came around slowly, but I did come around. The Jeep's heater helped, and so did a peanut butter sandwich and some room-temperature coffee from the thermos. It was still raining hard with no end in sight and we worried that the feeder creek we had to ford to get out of there could get too high to cross, but even then, it was another fifteen minutes before I stopped shaking enough to be able to drive. I could have handed the keys to either of my friends, but they didn't bring it up and I didn't think of it, possibly because I live with the unjustified belief that no one can handle my old Jeep as well as I can.

We never even strung up the rods.

12

WHISTLING GOPHERS

I was fishing with Mike Dvorak from Minnesota and Vince Zounek, my neighbor here in Colorado, two friends of mine who knew of each other but had never met before. I wasn't surprised that they hit it off. We all fly-fish—which puts us halfway there already—and beyond that we're just recognizable American guys of a certain vintage, not entirely unsophisticated, but not all that complicated, either.

Then there were the bamboo fly rods. We all admire them, own more of them than we need, fish with them often, and get tongue-tied when trying to explain to inquisitive bystanders what it is we like about them. Some are honestly curious, but most just can't get past the high prices that are charged for some of these rods and have become what another friend calls "whistling gophers" who ask, "What's one of those go fer?" and then whistle loudly when they hear the answer.

Vince also builds them. He was always one of those hands-on perfectionists (he trained as a machinist and is a good finish carpenter, among other skills) so he isn't as intimidated as most would be by the prospect of working to tolerances of a few thousandths of an inch using hand tools. (Those, by the way, are the kind of traits that describe every rod maker I've ever known.) By the time I met him, he had already made his first rod at a seminar in Arkansas. As first rods go, it was better than most, but although he fished with it from time to time and didn't hate it, he wasn't all that pleased with it, either, and thought he could do better. That was the inflection point where someone like Vince decides to put in the time and effort it takes to perfect the craft, while someone like me long ago decided to buy my rods from people like him. Likewise, when I have a job that requires a tractor, I'll hire a guy, but Vince buys the tractor and does it himself.

Like all craftsmen, Vince has become a connoisseur of raw materials by necessity: in this case, cork for grips, hardwood for reel seats, nickel silver for hardware, silk thread for wraps, and especially bamboo. There are more than a thousand species worldwide, but the kind that interests rod makers is the *Arundinaria amabilis* that's cultivated on the wet but well-drained slopes along the Sui River in southern China. Americans call it Tonkin bamboo; the Chinese call it tea stick. When it's dried, it's straw-colored, strong enough to be used for scaffolding, and has an almost musical hardness that makes bamboo wind chimes ring like a xylophone, but it retains its natural ability to bend deeply in the wind or under a blanket of snow and then spring back straight. It's as if this one species of bamboo evolved for no other reason than to be used to make fly rods. Unlike elephant tusks or cocaine, it's perfectly legal to buy and sell bamboo, but it's pricey, availability is unreliable, the quality can vary wildly, and you have to know the right people to find it, so that getting a shipment of the stuff can seem slightly illicit.

A rod shop only has to be large enough to manhandle a 12-foot culm of bamboo, even if you have to take it outside to turn it around. It'll contain adjustable planning forms, planes, a honing guide, a glue binder, depth gauge, lathe, drill press, vise, heat gun, assorted hand tools like a fine-tooth saw, and often something startlingly clunky, like the wood mallet and crudely sharpened screwdriver one rod maker I know uses to split culms or the old gym locker customized as a dustless drying cabinet used by another. There'll probably also be a thirty-five-gallon garbage can filled with the fine, curly bamboo shavings that are useful as mulch or to start fires in a woodstove. If you wandered in not knowing what it was for, you could wonder what goes on there.

I don't remember if Mike knew beforehand that Vince built rods or if he learned of it on that trip. These things are just in the air, although among fishermen the fact that someone makes bamboo rods would come up pretty early in the conversation. Anyway, when Mike asked about the rods, Vince handed him one—a 7½-foot, 5-weight—and told him to go ahead and fish it that day. This was the same soft sell I'd seen other rod builders use. Words fail when it comes to describing the action of a fly rod, so why not just let the test drive do the talking? The conditions on that trip couldn't have been better for it. This was in October, on a good tailwater fishery in the headwaters of the Colorado River with multiple hatches lasting from ten till three most days, tailor-made for light bamboo rods and the floating lines and small dry flies that show them off best.

I also don't remember if Mike ordered a rod while we were still on the river or if he waited till he got home. In the same situation,

I'll take a week or two to try to talk myself out of spending the money for yet another rod, and then when I can't, I'll call the guy—who, incidentally, never sounds surprised to hear from me. Most rod makers can tell when you're hooked, but understand they might have to give you some line and let you play yourself out before they land you. I do remember that Mike wasn't especially in the market for a new rod, but we all know what that means. Right off the top of my head I can name four rods I bought when I wasn't in the market, and if I pondered it for a while I could probably come up with a few more.

At this point, Vince had a couple of standard models, would accept orders, and had a business card in lieu of a catalog or website—essentially operating by word of mouth, which still works in an environment of cottage industries and avid devotees—but he had too many other irons in the fire to build rods full-time. So the one stipulation to Mike's order was that he have the rod by spring. It's a consideration. A rod maker once told me that something like four hundred separate operations go into the making of a bamboo fly rod. Many of them are time-consuming in their own right and some also require downtime for drying and curing, so delivery dates can stretch out, especially when the builder has a dozen other projects in the works, plus fishing. And no one in his right mind would buy a rod from someone who doesn't go fishing.

I've known a handful of rod makers—some well, others in passing—and no two of them went at it the same way. Some learned the craft from more experienced builders and others were largely self-taught. Some kept pretty much to themselves while others went to every conclave they could find and flitted around the online community of rod builders and collectors like hummingbirds. Some were self-proclaimed hobbyists who were eventually talked into making rods for a few friends, and that's as far as it ever went. Others tinkered with rods on the side for years and then got serious when they retired, recognizing rod making as a better way to supplement Social Security than being a greeter at Walmart. Others took up rod building by way of a conscious career change, with varying degrees of success. A dedicated handful go to their shops every morning and bang out rods at the rate of as many as forty a year. Most others keep more forgiving schedules, and one builder in Tennessee told me he just tries to sell enough rods in a year to pay for his health insurance.

The rod Vince made for Mike is based on one the late John Bradford made for me in 2002. He called it the "Stage IV," a reference to a long, involved private joke between us that I won't go into. John told me at the time that it was made on the famous Payne 197 taper that he'd "tweaked a little," although he had the good sense not to say he had "improved" it. He didn't specify *how* he'd tweaked it, correctly assuming I wouldn't understand what he was talking about. Sometime later, Vince was busy learning about rod tapers by casting the best rods he could get his hands on and putting a serious study on the ones he liked best. He'd cast them, measure the dimensions of their tapers, cast them again, and stand at a distance to watch others cast them, all the time fixing in his mind how the tapers related to the rod's action. Do this enough and you become like a musician who can look at a written score and hear the music in his head. He did that with several of my rods, but he held on to that Bradford for so long, I began to wonder if I'd ever get it back.

At least on paper, determining a rod's taper is a logical proce-dure. You take the measurements off the existing rod with a microm-eter, make an educated guess as to how much to subtract to allow for the varnish (two-thousandths of an inch is the usual standard), and so arrive at the actual dimensions of the unfinished shaft. Then you do the calculations that translate a hexagonal rod into the six triangular-shaped splines that, when glued together, will make the taper. Those are the measurements you set your planning form to.

But in reality, reproducing a rod isn't as straightforward as it sounds. I don't own a 7½-foot Payne made by Jim Payne himself—they've always been beyond my budget—but I've cast a few of them, as well as any number of others that were built on the same iconic taper. If this were a simple matter of reverse engineering, all those rods would have cast the same, but they didn't because there are too many variables. Whether or not the bamboo was heat treated—and if so, how, and how much—makes a difference; so does the glue used to fasten the splines together, so does the node spacing, and so does the culm of bamboo that was used, which a maker selects knowing that a big culm has larger, stiffer fibers than a smaller one. And so on and so forth. All that assumes the absolute accuracy of your micrometer and the settings on your planning form, neither of which is a foregone conclusion.

There are also imponderables, like the belief among some that a bamboo rod mellows with age and use, the way an already good violin will sound even better after being played for a hundred years than it did when it was new. Offhand, I can't think of a way to verify that, but I've always thought it sounded right.

For that matter, rod builders are hopeless tinkerers who are unable or unwilling to leave well enough alone, and so they don't. Over the years I've met two guys who claimed to be faithfully reproducing the tapers of classic rod builders—Everett Garrison in one case, Goodwin Granger in the other—but everyone else tweaks and fiddles compulsively, fine-tuning the already fine-tuned, even if a sympathetic but objective observer like me can't tell the difference. They remind me of some editors I've known who'll redraft a perfectly good sentence for no other reason than that redrafting sentences is in their job description. This is further complicated by the counterintuitive fact that a few thousandths of an inch more or less in one place on a blank won't make much difference at all, while in another place it can either improve or ruin the action.

That's why there's an alchemy attached to the work of particular rod makers that's hard to put a finger on and impossible to reproduce accurately. So a Payne becomes a Bradford, which in turn becomes a Zounek, and although they all seem familiar, they're not identical. (For that matter, that Payne taper which served as the benchmark didn't come out of nowhere, either. Payne was a second-generation rod builder whose father's roots reached back as far as Hiram Leonard in the 1800s.)

It's that sense of familiarity that always attracts me to rods. Among the light bamboo fly rods of mine that Vince looked at are 7½-footers by Bradford, Leonard, F. E. Thomas, and Granger; 7-foot, 9-inch rods by Mike Clark and Walter Babb; and a pair of 8-foot, 4-weights by Thomas and Charlie Jenkins. They're not all the same, but they do all share the quick, tippy dry-fly action that's characteristic of the Golden Age bamboo rods, so that after your first two or three casts with any one of them, you get the friendly feeling that you've been fishing it for twenty years. (Rods that are described as "demanding" are fine for connoisseurs, but I'd rather they make their demands of someone else.) It's possible that none of them are perfect fly rods in any objective sense, but any of them could be, in the right hands. Charlie Daniels once said that there's no difference between a fiddle and a violin; it's all in how it's played.

The technical voodoo behind the best bamboo rods remains a mystery to me, as it should. All I need to know is that at its best, craftsmanship goes beyond mere do-it-yourself projects and begins to flirt with artistry, just as the best rods make the leap from useful tool to beautiful instrument. There's also an element of sentiment to it. I know or have known some of the makers whose rods I

own—some of whom are no longer with us—and that makes a difference. It's hard to explain, but as someone who once kept laying hens,
I can testify that already good free-range eggs taste even better when
you know the chickens that laid them. No, I didn't give them names;
I referred to them collectively as "the girls" to distinguish them from
my cantankerous rooster.

When I first got interested in bamboo rods, I was just another
whistling gopher floored by what some of them cost, so I made do
with good old rods by makers who hadn't become collectible yet. But
as time went by, it became obvious that some of those makers were
underrated at the time, and most of them did eventually become collectible, so as it turned out, I've gotten more than my money's worth.
(Benign neglect is the only investment strategy I understand.) As I
learned more about what it took to make them—not just the one
rod, but the long, uphill slog of learning and perfecting the craft—
the prices started to look more reasonable, until I began to wonder
why they don't cost more than they do. As the old saying goes, "You
couldn't pay me enough . . ."

Before Mike's rod got shipped off, I cast it in the pasture in front
of Vince's house. (I didn't think Mike would mind and he didn't.) It
was what I expected: friendly, familiar, forgiving, effortless—pick a
word—with the right balance and heft and just the right combination
of give and resistance to make a fly line feel weightless. My friend Ed
Engle once said the difference between graphite and bamboo fly rods
is that graphite shoots line, while bamboo *casts* it. As a description of
something indescribable, I thought that came pretty damned close.

I haven't cast all the rods Vince has made, but I've cast a lot of
them and have fished with a couple, knowing that you'll learn more
about a rod in a few hours on a trout stream than you will in a few
minutes on the lawn. Vince likes to try them out on me, not because
I'm such a great fly caster, but because he thinks that if I didn't like

a rod, I wouldn't pull my punches. In fact, if it ever happened I probably *would* pull my punches, but he'd be able to tell.

The day after Mike got the rod, he took it to one of the spring creeks near where he lives and caught, among other fish, a nice fat brown trout and sent a photo of it to Vince. Two photos, actually. One was of the trout and the rod and the other was a close-up of the signature wraps on the rod—a warm golden brown with a reddish/orange tag—next to the trout's adipose fin to show that the colors matched almost exactly. I know that rod makers sometimes add subtle touches like that on purpose, even though most of us will never notice. John Bradford once spent weeks formulating a wood stain that would make his maple reel seat spacers exactly match the color of the toasted bamboo on his rods. It's not the kind of thing that jumps out at you and I knew John well enough to understand that it spoke more to his private sense of excellence than to any ideas he might have had about marketing, although if the customer thought, even subliminally, that the rod seemed somehow more *finished* than most, that was okay, too.

But when I asked Vince if he'd purposely chosen the wrap colors on his rod to match the adipose fin on a brown trout, he said no, although he did think it was a nice coincidence.

13

KOOTENAI

This was the ideal introduction to a new river. Dave Blackburn picked me up at the airport in Kalispell and we drove the hour and a half to his place on the Kootenai River near Libby, Montana, roughly sixty miles as the crow flies south of Canada and about twenty-five miles east of the Idaho state line. Dave had fishermen booked for an afternoon float, so he dropped me off at the cabin he was letting me use for a few nights and said he'd swing back by that evening and we'd see about getting dinner.

I did the usual short-term nesting—which amounted to tossing my gear in a corner and figuring out how the coffeemaker worked—and then stepped out on the porch for a look at the river. It was a stone's throw away, flowing at 6,000 cubic feet per second now in the third week of September and making that insistent rushing sound you almost don't hear but would miss if it stopped.

Down at the water's edge with a fly rod, I studied the choppy run in front of the cabin and decided it was as good a place as any to start. Up close the water was clear, but at a distance the same low clouds that obscured the surrounding mountains turned the river a chilly, dishwater gray. A freight train was passing along the far bank, grinding along slowly through the canyon. This would turn out to be a regular thing, every few hours, day and night, for as long as I was there—hoppers full of coal and tankers filled with crude oil —but it wouldn't bother me. I've been nuts for trains since childhood and when adults asked what I wanted to be when I grew up, I alternated between cowboy and railroad brakeman. (I wanted to be a brakeman instead of an engineer because I thought the brakeman lived in the caboose.) So I not only don't mind, but indeed kind of like, the clacking and rumbling of trains and their mournful horns, especially when they're muffled by distance and the sound of a river.

This was the kind of cool, overcast day that trout like, but the Kootenai was enigmatic. There were no insects on or above the water, no rises, boils, or subsurface flashes that I could see, and Dave had either forgotten to fill me in or had paid me the compliment of assuming I could figure it out myself. It was the moment every fisherman faces when a new river might as well be a locked door with a sign saying "authorized personnel only."

Since there hadn't yet been a hard frost to kill them, I thought there should still be grasshoppers around—and trout love grasshoppers—so I tied on a size 12 Dave's Hopper and fished up the run, starting close and working out as far as I could cast and still get a good drift. Nothing. So I added a Pheasant Tail dropper to the dry fly and fished through the same water. Again, nothing.

I tried a size 14 Elk Hair caddis—a fly that could work on any trout river in North America—and fished it downstream, first with a dead drift and then on a second pass with the little skitters and twitches that are intended to suggest a living insect.

When that didn't produce, I marched through four more fly changes in quick succession, with my confidence diminishing along with the length of my leader: first the kind of big, bushy dry fly Ted Leeson calls a "Dust Bunny," then a smaller dry fly, then a stone fly nymph, and then a Woolly Bugger. Not sure what was I trying to accomplish. Administer a multiple-choice quiz? Impress the trout with the scope of my fly selection?

Then I took a break and a deep breath and in answer to the obvious question, What would you do back home? I tied on a brace of soft hackles, swung the flies down and across current, and got a fat little rainbow that jumped twice and missed two others. It was as simple as that.

Now I felt I was onto something, but I also thought I'd about worn out this run, so I walked upstream to look for new water. Dave had described this stretch and I easily found the gate through the barbed-wire fence and, a little farther up the bank, the two pines leaning together that marked the Home Pool. It looked promising: three to four feet deep with a walking-speed current flowing over a bottom littered with small boulders, like a textbook illustration of holding water.

There was a steep bank here with willows and pines that blocked a back cast, so I used an imperfect but adequate one-handed double Spey cast, swung the pool methodically, and picked up a few more rainbows as fat, silvery, and acrobatic as the first one, but somewhat bigger.

Waiting for Dave back at the cabin, I took a few minutes to examine the place. It was clearly built by someone who knew what they were doing, made of twenty-two-inch-diameter pine logs that Dave told me later had been cut on a firewood permit and skidded out whole. (No law says you have to burn the wood.) The logs had been peeled with a draw knife, so I couldn't tell if they were lodgepole or ponderosa, but I guessed lodgepole because of their straightness and uniformity. The notches at the corners locked solidly, the chinking was snug, the plank floor fit flush, doors and windows were tight, and there wasn't a crack or a gap anywhere. I thought that if it didn't burn down, the river didn't wash it away, and it wasn't bulldozed to make room for condos, this cabin would still be here in a hundred years.

When Dave showed up that evening, he asked, "How'd you do?"

"Got a few," I said.

"On what?" he asked.

"Soft hackles."

"Yup," he said. "That sounds right."

The next morning we had breakfast at a café in Libby where the waitress greeted Dave by name and brought him his "usual": a pile of eggs, sausages, and potatoes big enough to feed two grown men. We were with Taylor, whom Dave introduced as a new guide—not new to guiding, but new to the Kootenai—that Dave wanted to check out on this lower float before sending him out with clients.

We were hoping for Blue-wing Olive mayflies and the day was right for it—chilly, with a low, gray ceiling and a light rain just a notch or two above a drizzle: a morning anyone but a fly fisher would describe as "gloomy." At the put-in I tied on my own size 20 parachute Olive for the floater and one of Dave's patterns for the dropper: a small, sparse wet fly with a few wood duck fibers for a tail, the thinnest possible dubbed body, and just a single turn of ruffed grouse hackle. It was exactly the kind of nondescript little nothing of a fly that often works, if only because there isn't enough of it for a trout to find fault with.

There were only a few sporadic rises that morning, but I picked up a couple of rainbows while Dave and Taylor ran the shuttle and the rest of the day passed in much the same way. The hatch wasn't thick, but mayflies sputtered off, the fish were looking up, and Dave and I hooked trout here and there while Taylor rowed and listened to Dave's running monologue on how to guide this stretch.

There are more similarities than differences between trout rivers, so most of it was self-evident, but there were the usual spots that looked good, but weren't, as well as the sleepers that *didn't* look good, but could have their moments. That was interspersed with a season's worth of hatches and fly patterns, plus casting angles, good lunch spots, local history, big fish stories, and other things a guide should know. It was too much to absorb at a single sitting, but the relevant snatches of it that weren't obvious would resurface as needed.

They were engrossed enough in their conversation to make me feel pleasantly on my own, but these guys are both experienced guides who instinctively keep the flies in their peripheral vision, so whenever I'd get a take they'd both say "set," more or less in unison— melody and harmony. It's a reflex most guides come by honestly, having watched countless clients sleepwalk though perfectly good eats. Sometimes the heads-up is merely redundant; other times it can actually throw off your timing—which in my case is none too flawless as it is—and occasionally it's helpful. A few days later, Dave would say "set" and then, when I came up tight on a trout, add, "Sorry, I know you know when to set." I appreciated the sentiment, but in that case, I'd been lost in thought and would have missed the fish if he hadn't said anything. Not that it would have mattered. There were plenty of trout and if fishing teaches you anything, it's how to shrug off failure and cast again.

I'd met Taylor for the first time that morning, but Dave and I go back to the Elk River in British Columbia, not all that far north of here, where we met and fished together in what we both guess must have been about 1990. I remember thinking at the time that he knew what he was doing. No telling what he thought of me. We've seen each other most years since then at the fly-fishing show in Denver, where he mans the booth promoting his Kootenai River fly shop and guide service and plays banjo in the food court at lunchtime. (He said recently, "Fly-fishing and bluegrass just naturally go together." It's an opinion not everyone shares, but you get what he means.) At many of those shows we'd idly talked about fishing together again, this time on the Kootenai, and at the last one I finally said, "Well, let's just do it then," like a man accepting a challenge. No idea why it took us so long. We're both busy, but not *that* busy.

When Dave and I first met, he was already established in this valley between the Purcell and Cabinet mountain ranges. He arrived here with a degree in forestry from West Virginia University, but found he could make better money felling trees than marking them and that also left time in the evenings to guide fishermen. He'd started out as a live minnow guy and would once have said there was no reason to fish any other way, but by then he'd made the transition to fly casting. He and his wife, Tammy, bought the house where they still live in 1983. (It's the home in Home Pool.) Originally it was on three acres, but they've since parlayed that into a spread covering fifty-eight acres, with a barn that's been converted to a bunkhouse and several guest cabins. There's also a saloon and restaurant called the River Bend with a fly shop conveniently attached and a guide service that can run as many as six boats a day "if all the stars are aligned properly." Dave also plays banjo in a bluegrass band called Boulder Creek, a group of local musicians you could call amateurs in the purest sense of doing it as much for love as for money. They play gigs here and there and can often be heard at the River Bend, where, presumably, they don't have any trouble getting booked.

Dave doesn't seem especially harried considering the number of balls he keeps in the air, although he *is* busy enough that you wonder when he finds time to practice the banjo. Technically he qualifies as an entrepreneur, but in the end he seems happy enough just to be "the fishing guy" and that's how people know him. On the drive up from the airport we were stopped for road construction by a woman holding a stop sign and wearing an orange hard hat with Viking horns glued to it. She ambled over to Dave's open window, said hello, and asked if the kokanee run had reached the snagging hole yet. He assured her it had and after a few more pleasantries she waved us through.

Of course, it hasn't all gone smoothly. In the late 1970s and '80s, Dave was part of the opposition to a proposed hydroelectric project on the Kootenai and you can guess how that went. Stand in the way of profit and progress on environmental grounds and you're at least a tree-hugging hippie if not an outright communist. The project was eventually scrapped when government policies changed in favor of habitat protection, but before that there were hard feelings, harsh words, and even vandalism, the kind of things that, in a small Western town, are never actually forgotten, but that can be put on a back burner and left to simmer harmlessly while everyone gets on with their lives.

Late on the afternoon of that first day, we took out within sight of the Idaho state line. This had been a fairly placid float, but then the lowest elevation in Montana—1,820 feet—is at that exact spot where the river enters Idaho. There was only one gnarly spot where Dave took the oars to show Taylor how to negotiate it this first time. You could picture it as a bow and arrow, with a wide bend in the Kootenai as the bow and a smaller river called the Yaak coming in at a more or less right angle as the arrow.

Where the currents of the two rivers combined, the water picked up speed and volume and slammed against the cliff face on the outside of the bend. It seemed obvious that you should come in tight to the inlet of the Yaak and pull across into the calm eye of the pool, and that's how Dave did it, but he said some fishermen had once been pinned against that cliff in high water and drowned, so it was worth a demonstration.

So this, finally, was the Kootenai, at least the stretch of it that loops south into Montana and then flows back north into British Columbia across the chimney of Idaho. I'd never been on it before, but I'd fished several of its tributaries on the Canadian side—the Elk, Bull, Skookumchuck, St. Mary's, and Wigwam, for west slope cutthroats and bull trout—and I'd fished the Columbia for redbands below where the Kootenai enters it at Castlegar, British Columbia, plus several other Columbia tributaries closer to the coast for steelhead. This is one way—spanning more than thirty years—to begin to get a hint at the enormity and perpetual motion of rivers.

For the next few days, Dave and I floated with his German shorthair, Maisy, a high-strung, high-stepping, nine-year-old pointer. ("That's like 'Daisy' but with an *M*," Dave said.) I'd met Maisy when I got in the first day and for the rest of my stay she came to my cabin to say hello first thing every morning, either because she recognized a dog lover or just as an excuse to sprint the hundred yards across the meadow from home and, after a pat on the head and a kind word, dash back to run off a small fraction of her breed's inexhaustible energy.

Maisy is a good girl, but I wouldn't describe her as a good fishing dog. At put-ins and take-outs she'd wander off looking for game birds, following the irresistible call of her breeding, and have to be whistled up. She was calm enough in the boat—in a pent-up sort of way—until I'd hook a fish, at which point she'd begin to come unglued. There would be whining and pacing and, as I played the fish to within netting range, she'd perch with her front feet on the gunnel and lean out so far that, four or five times a day, she'd fall in. Then I'd have to give my fish line while Dave lifted the dog back on board, where she'd shake off and go right back to leaning out over the gunnel, more likely to fall in again now because she was shivering and her paws were wet. By the end of the first day I was thinking of Albert Einstein's famous definition of insanity as "doing the same thing over and over again and expecting different results."

In one braided stretch I switched to a brace of weighted nymphs and caught a bunch of whitefish, nice big fat ones, and learned that Maisy isn't a trout snob; she gets just as excited over whitefish. At a deep bridge pool I swung a weighted streamer and got a heavy pull, but didn't hook up. Maybe it was a bull trout, a protected species here that you might catch by accident but aren't supposed to target. To catch them legally, you'd have to drive across the border into Canada.

But mostly I fished Dave's sparse little soft hackle as a dropper behind a dry fly and caught fish after fish on it. (I've since copied the pattern and have done well with it at home, too.) The best drift was steeply down and across current ahead of the boat, keeping a line just tight enough to swing the flies ever so slowly. That little bit of insect-like action was just enough to convince the fish that the fly was alive and edible. Or so I assumed. Whenever you're catching trout, you flatter yourself that you've read their minds.

Naturally, the best day of fishing was our last, when we had to get off the river by lunchtime so I could make my afternoon flight out of Kalispell. By then the rain had stopped, the clouds were more white than gray, the sky had broken out into scattered patches of blue, and the mayflies were already hatching when we launched. Instead of blind fishing likely looking water or casting to occasional solitary risers, we were working pods of feeding trout, and most of them would eat Dave's little soft hackle as if they'd been waiting for it all morning. It was hard to tear ourselves away at the appointed time, but that kind of thing happens so often that I no longer feel cheated by inflexible schedules and the hectic lives that make them seem necessary. After some effort, I'm now able to be grateful to have had that long morning float with leaping rainbows, a friend on the oars, and a wet dog.

Getting dropped off at the airport after a fishing trip is a poignant moment, especially in the fall, when another season is winding down before you're ready. You can't put your finger on exactly what it is, but you can't shake the feeling that something has been left undone. We had dropped the boat off at Dave's place, but he brought the dog and a shotgun along so he could stop on the way back to sneak in an hour or two of grouse hunting, and I caught myself wishing I could have watched Maisy point some birds. I think I'd remember her as less of a goofball now if I'd seen her in the flattering light of what she does best.

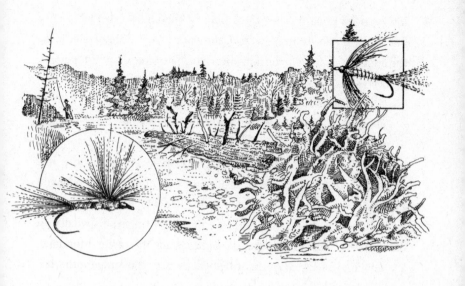

14

DRAKES

It's a shortcut that, driving north from my house, drops you off midway up the canyon, eliminating more than an hour from the long route that puts you in at the bottom, but it doesn't feel short. The trip still takes a couple of hours, almost all of it on slow, winding two-lanes that get more serpentine the farther north you go, right down to blind, 15-mile-an-hour switchbacks and rumbling cattle guards. It's the kind of road that leads to fishing.

Two things always occur to me on this drive: One is that a common cause of accidents on mountain roads is tourist drivers straying over the centerline as they rubberneck the scenery. The other is a dumb tourist story I heard years ago from a fly shop owner in Idaho. He'd just given a man from New York directions to a fishing spot. "Take the first two-track on the left after you pass the cattle guard," he said. The guy thanked him and started for the door, then turned and asked, "What kind of uniform does a cattle guard wear?"

This road gains altitude gradually the whole way—starting in uplifted sandstone rimrock and easing gradually into forested foothills—and then loses it abruptly as you snake down off a low saddle into the river canyon. Landmarks along the way include a stretch of fence with pickets made from old downhill skis and a fund-raising sign for the local volunteer fire department shaped like a thermometer with a red line showing how close they are to their goal. It's been there for years and for that whole time the temperature has stayed pretty chilly. You know you're getting close to the river when you pass a hand-painted sign saying, "Caution, dumb (old) dogs on road," and then, around the next bend, another sign that mentions children as an afterthought.

Turning left at the two-lane blacktop that parallels the river past its headwaters, there's still another forty-five minutes to go before you reach the stretch where the Green Drake hatch is at its best and I'm glad to see every mile of it. There are no fewer than sixty roadside miles of river here and most fishermen drive up from the mouth of the canyon, passing countless turnouts overlooking luxurious water, so many of them stop to fish before they get to where I'm going.

It's not that this hatch is a secret. Most of the fishermen I've talked to here know about the Drakes, although they'll rarely mention them first, in case you don't. I once asked a man I met on the river what he was getting 'em on.

"Size twelve dry fly," he said vaguely.

I said, "So, a Drake then."

130

He looked away upriver, then down at his boots and replied, "Well . . . yeah."

The fly shop that calls this river home has Drake patterns in its fly bins and at least one guide (a friend of mine) who understands these big mayflies better than most, but for some reason the Drakes don't appear on their hatch chart. It's probably just an oversight. The Drake hatch here isn't one of those famous hatches that lure tourists from far away, although more people know about it than some of us would like. But then, the days when fly-fishing was a quirky little backwater that allowed secrets to be kept are so far in the past now that newer participants don't believe they ever existed. "Imagine a world with a fraction of the fishermen and without cell phones or the internet," I'll say, and they'll stand there blinking, drawing a blank, and wondering why they stopped to talk to this old guy in the first place.

When I started fishing this hatch, it would often come off well for a few hours sometime between 11 a.m. and four. The water was never blanketed with bugs, but on good days they would be thick enough to trigger pods of risers and odd singles: a Drake hatch like you read about in the fishing books. It wasn't always dependable—midsummer hatches are easily put off by heat waves and thunderstorms—but if you spent enough days on the water, the odds of eventually hitting it right were in your favor.

More recently, the hatch has begun to sputter. For the last few seasons the duns have been coming off in odd flurries, a few at a time, here and there along the stretch of river that's known to some as the Drake water. Half an hour of that, then a dead spell, and then another small flurry, possibly on a different stretch of river, as if the hatch were trying to sneak off without either the trout or the fishermen noticing. Some say the Drake population itself is dwindling, while others say no, there are just as many as there ever were, but the way they dribble off now only makes it seem like there are fewer.

People have naturally wondered why this would be. Maybe it's just a natural cycle; up for a while, then down for a while, like careers, marriages, or the stock market. Or maybe it's the cumulative effect of climate change that has turned the summers progressively hotter over the last thirty years or so—one of thousands of answers to the question "What possible difference could a few extra degrees make?"

Trout will still eat the duns even when there aren't a lot of them on the water, although when they're not rising steadily, the fish are harder to locate. But if you read water well, you can guess where they might be and why: in the tails of pools; in the moderate, foamy currents you could think of as chow lines; and in soft water beside faster currents where a trout can lie in wait without much effort and then dart out to grab flies drifting by. This can be a setup. When they've been fished for, trout get suspicious of flies, but when they move for one in fast current, the decision has been made and there's no time for last-minute second thoughts. Trout Psychology 101.

Fly patterns are anyone's guess. I have a few favorites arranged in a personal hierarchy and so does everyone else. Bushy and sparse, high-floating and low-floating, and some old-timers—as well as others who are just old at heart—stick with a size 12 Adams as a kind of take-it-or-leave-it gesture. Size 12 is the nearly universal standard, but I've talked to fishermen who tie their imitations slightly oversized to make them stand out and others who tie them slightly smaller than the naturals to help them blend in. The reasoning always sounds impeccable and anyone who ever catches a fish believes their theory has been proven.

I went up this year as soon as the seasonal timing and the stream flow coincided in what I thought was an auspicious way and parked in a pullout on the outside of a big, sweeping bend in the river. There was another car there ahead of me, an SUV with a Trout Unlimited bumper sticker and a rod caddy on the roof. I thought about moving, but this is a spot I like and if you get indecisive you can end up driving up and down the river all day instead of fishing. Anyway, the fisherman was nowhere in sight either upstream or down, so I guessed that the water had been rested enough.

I rigged up with my first-choice Green Drake parachute and added a soft hackle emerger as a dropper for good measure. All I'd heard through the grapevine was that the hatch *should* be on, so this was somewhere between an act of faith and wishful thinking. The big bend pool right at the turnout seemed like a good place to start. Sometimes these spots are good because everyone assumes they've been pounded to death and so they pass them by. It's not a sure thing, but it's always worth at least a few casts. And this is interesting water, with the big rotating eye of the eddy itself and a sneaky little tongue of current that sweeps back upstream against the riprap of the roadbed. As I waded into position, I saw one Drake dun drift by on the edge of the main current and another struggling along in the air a bit farther downstream. Smaller mayflies lift off effortlessly, but the big Drakes seem to work harder to get airborne, like Canada geese. These hatches are so iconic that sometimes just seeing the insects amounts to a small victory, regardless of what happens next.

I got one fat 14-inch brown trout in the eddy, two more that I had spotted rising in the back current along the far bank, and missed a fourth, probably by being too quick on the trigger when I set the hook. Working my way on upstream after that, I saw only a few mayflies and no more rising trout, but I got one fish in the soft edge of a riffle, missed one in the tail of a foamy glide, and got one more nice brown from the pressure wave in front of a midstream boulder.

Things slowed down after that, and I was taking a break on the bank to think about my next move when a fisherman came trudging downstream—the driver of the SUV, I assumed. As he passed I asked, "How'd you do up there?"

"I got a few until the goddamned bugs stopped hatching," he said. "Then I couldn't *buy* a goddamned fish. Goddamn it!"

This would be one of those guys who say they fish for relaxation.

Later I drove upstream to try another spot I know, but there was a fisherman just getting out of it when I pulled up. He had a bedraggled-looking Green Drake in his hook keeper and said he'd caught six fish. Gesturing over his shoulder he said, "It's all yours," and I thanked him, but it was a small run that had just been fished and the guy looked like he knew what he was doing, so I drove downstream and tried another spot I like. There were no rises and no bugs on the water, and after an hour or so it became obvious that it was over. I started thinking about supper and the slow drive back and pretty soon I was de-rigging at the pickup and starting for home.

The Drakes here begin around the third week of July and last in fits and starts through about the same time in August, a stretch of summer that's prone to hot spells, wildfires, and brief but violent monsoon thunderstorms. I went back up to fish the Drakes four or five more times, often enough that the drive began to seem like the commute to a dream job. It was irresistible. We've built up a whole belief system around these so-called super hatches: Mother's Day caddis, salmon flies, the night-hatching Hexagenia mayflies that are as big as hummingbirds, and all the smaller but still comparatively large mayflies known collectively as Drakes and distinguished by color: Green Drakes, Brown Drakes, Gray Drakes, etc. We've all heard the stories. These bugs are either so big or so prolific that they bring the largest trout in the river right up to the surface in a feeding frenzy that makes them lose their instinctive caution and become pushovers. Easy pickings. Fifty-fish days. It's like winning the lottery.

When I was fourteen years old, my father took me to lunch to meet an old man he knew. The guy was ancient and frail by then, but he'd been a lifelong hunter and fishermen—the two things I was crazy about—and he was brimming with stories as if he'd gone too long without an audience. Flocks of ducks that blackened the sky, bank-to-bank runs of salmon, stringers of 10-pound bass so heavy he had to get help to carry them up from the dock, that kind of thing. It was entertaining, except that the guy kept looking over at me sadly and saying, "Of course, you'll never get to see anything like that," and I came to hate him because I suspected he was right. The old days are the old days only because they're gone and won't be back.

The great trout stream hatches hold out hope for something like that—a glimpse of how things used to be—but there's no guarantee that they'll pan out. Maybe the bugs don't make an appearance or they only sputter off. Or maybe the hatch materializes in all its glory, but it's business as usual for the trout. Rather than losing their native caution, they're skittish as rabbits and overly critical of your flies. But even if it doesn't live up to the stories, you're nonetheless catching some fish during one of the legendary hatches and the weirdness of memory is such that when they ask about it back home you might hear yourself saying, "Yeah, I pretty much slaughtered 'em."

The last time I fished the Drakes was on one of the cloudy, drizzly days we so seldom get here in the summer. There were some other fishermen out, but the fair-weather types had stayed home, so there weren't many, and one turnout after another was vacant. So, I picked a spot I like and walked the thirty yards to a big spruce trunk that had washed aground on this gravel bar like a beached tanker in some long-past spring flood. It's been there for as long as I can remember, with its root ball festooned with spiderwebs and facing upstream into the prevailing wind and a look at those webs will give you the pretty accurate peek behind the scenes at what's been hatching lately. This time there were lots of midges, a few small, desiccated mayflies that may once have been Pale Morning Duns, a moth or two, and a pair of fairly fresh Green Drake duns.

It's fair to say that the hatch never came off that day, at least not where I was. I worked my way upstream casting a Green Drake parachute with a Harrop Emerger on a dropper to every place I thought a trout might be, and after an hour or so without seeing a dun on the water or getting a take, I stopped to rethink. I ended up switching to a weighted wet fly to get some depth, with the unweighted Harrop Emerger behind it on a dropper. After a few casts, I added two small split shot above the first fly to get more depth and a couple of swings later I picked up a fish.

It's possible that the rainy weather had put off the hatch, but it was also late enough in August that the whole thing could have been winding down to its end. Either way, it was an even bet that some trout would still pick up something that resembled the size, shape, and behavior of the swimming Drake emergers as long as they didn't have to move too far to get them. Or at least that's the accepted theory.

Working back downstream for the next hour or so, I got several more trout, missed a few others, and had waded out to the lip of a gravel bar so I could swing my flies in the big pool below. It was raining harder by then and I had the hood up on my rain slicker, which squashed the wide brim of my canvas hat down on the sides like earmuffs, so I didn't hear the moose coming up behind me until it had gotten entirely too close.

When I finally turned around there was a cow moose with a calf wading downstream toward me at a range of about thirty yards. To some, a cow moose with a calf doesn't look as ferocious as a bear with cubs, but she's every bit as short-tempered and her maternal instinct can be every bit as lethal. I got the impression that they had just spotted me (these animals are notoriously nearsighted) because they were still coming, but they had slowed their pace a little and the cow was squinting at me suspiciously while the calf had begun to prance around nervously. The near bank was blocked by moose and the far bank was across a deep, fast channel, so if this went wrong, I'd have to either step off into the pool or stand there and get stomped to a bloody pulp.

The cow kept coming but changed her angle slightly, or maybe that's where they were going anyway. It's in the nature of close calls that you never know exactly what happened or just how close you came. In the end, the cow splashed by, picking up speed, then turned and trotted across the gravel bank downstream and on into the woods with the calf high-stepping right behind her the whole way. They'd passed me at a range of . . . What? Fifteen yards? More? Less? It was close enough that I could see individual hairs on both animals and hear the mother's heavy breathing. I could have paced it off, but that didn't occur to me until later. I didn't feel especially shaken—no dry mouth or weak knees—but I may have been a little giddy from adrenaline because the whole episode struck me as tremendously funny and I stood there for a few minutes giggling idiotically.

After that I swung the few pools down to where I'd parked, but by then the rain was pounding, the air was cold, and the river had gone dead, so I walked back to my pickup, de-rigged quickly on the tailgate, and ducked into the cab and out of the weather. Then I poured a cup of coffee from the thermos, rolled down the window, and sat there watching the water for a while with errant raindrops dappling my shoulder and the coffee steaming. This river is designated "wild and scenic," and although it's hard to think of a river as wild when you can drive along it on a paved road, it definitely is a joy to look at and sometimes it's hard to tear yourself away even after you've torn yourself away.

15

SECOND HOME

I fell in the river. I don't mean I stumbled or waded too deep and shipped a little water or any of the other minor mishaps that befall fishermen. I mean I *fell:* a real silent-movie, heels-in-the-air pratfall worthy of Charlie Chaplin. One second, I was upright, dry, and in control of my destiny; the next I was in the river up to my armpits, wondering how I got there while both hip boots filled like ice-water balloons. Later a friend asked, "How'd it happen?" I said, "If I knew how it happened, I wouldn't have done it that way, would I?"

This was in March, on a gray day in the last official week of winter, with spitting snow carried on a chilly breeze, so by the time I made sure my rod wasn't broken, emptied my hippers, and trudged back to the pickup with my socks squishing obscenely in my boots, a deep, chattering chill had set in and I had to sit in the cab with the heater blasting until I warmed up enough to plan my next move.

There wasn't really a hatch that day—there were no trout rising and only a few small mayfly duns popping off now and then—but these were the first mayflies I'd seen in months and I couldn't resist tying on a dry fly after a long winter. I didn't have high hopes. I just thought I'd enjoy the prettiness of the cast, mend, and drift for a while before getting serious with a pair of weighted nymphs. But then just by blind casting to likely looking water I managed to raise and hook two brown trout against the odds. That was after blowing the set on the first take because it was the last thing I expected.

Then, as my fly drifted through a slick behind a rock, a good-sized rainbow rose to within a fraction of an inch of it, with his nose almost touching the hook, before he reconsidered and turned away without so much as rippling the surface. It took less than a second, but still seemed to happen in a kind of visionary slow motion.

I made one more cast before I stopped myself. I knew that if a trout doesn't like your fly on the first drift, he probably won't like it any better on subsequent tries, and that pounding him for too long will just make him go away. But this was a good fish that had betrayed at least a passing interest, so my plan was to wade to the bank, rest him long enough for his wariness to subside, and then come back and show him a different fly. Maybe my attention wandered at a crucial moment, or maybe I just hit a slick rock, but that's when I went in.

My doctor worries when I fall (she's motherly that way) and thinks it has something to do with my age and bad knees. To her credit, she's never advised me to act my age, but she *has* asked, "What did you do this time?" in the tone of an exasperated parent. I'd been in to see her the previous August after a fall on a boulder-strewn tributary creek. I was stalking a rising trout, stepped on a rock I didn't expect to be loose, and went down, bashing my shoulder hard enough to get an X-ray to look for bone chips, but saving my rod. I explained then that I don't fall any more often now than I did thirty years ago (I've never been graceful and anyone can step on a loose rock) and I compared fly-fishing to other sports, like skiing, where the occasional spill is just part of the game. Still, she asked, "Why do it?" So I stole a line from George Mallory, and said, "Because it's there," and she nodded as if that answered her question.

My pickup has a good heater, so I soon had warm air blowing on my pant legs, where I'd rolled down my hip boots, and all the stuff in my pockets that shouldn't have gotten wet, but did, was spread out to dry on the seat next to me. To kill time, I was listening to the news on the radio. The news that day was no more cheerful than usual, but at least the sketchy reception in the canyon made it seem far away.

The last time I'd sat warming up in the pickup along this same river was five months earlier, on a similar day in late October of the previous year. (After a while, the cab of a pickup with the heater running begins to feel like a second home.) The fall hatches had been winding down through a spate of unseasonably warm, bluebird days, the kind of lovely Indian summer weather that everyone except a fly fisherman likes. Friends and I went up to the river anyway. By October, the end of fishing for another year is in sight and you don't feel like wasting whatever time you have left before winter settles in. Also, like most fishermen, we consider ourselves problem solvers and a few trout rising halfheartedly to a smattering of tiny flies in low, clear water under a bright sun is about as hard as it gets.

There's the usual struggle with minute fly patterns and nearly invisible tippets, wearing magnifier glasses and standing at just the right angle to get the fly in sunlight against the contrast of a shady background in order to thread the eye of the hook. Then there's the usual squinting to pick the speck of the fly's white wing out of the dozens of similar specks in a tongue of foamy current. Years spent staring at rivers will teach you to discern the infinitesimal difference in color and texture between foam and feather, and on those occasions when, at the end of the drift when you pick up the fly and find that you'd been watching the wrong speck, you shrug, cast again, and squint even harder.

Of course, most mayfly wings are dull gray, so tying flies with white wings for better visibility is already a compromise, and some have gone the full distance with wings tied of rug yarn dyed hot pink or chartreuse. Those flies do work—apparently the trout don't mind them as much as I think they should—and it's comforting to think they're one more thing to resort to when the time comes, along with even stronger magnifier glasses.

This makes fly-fishing sound maddening and sometimes it is, which may be the whole point. We wallow in the difficulty of it, whether we're the heroes of our own stories or the butt of our own jokes. On days when we manage to catch a few fish in difficult conditions, we brag about our skill as anglers. On the days when we don't, we drive ourselves quietly nuts for a few hours and then go home contented and refreshed and shaking our heads over what an odd sport this is.

It's mostly a matter of timing, and fishermen are forever studying the mosaic of circumstances, hoping to get the jump on a few hours of good fishing. It's rarely just one thing, although sometimes when the other elements are close enough to right, it's just one more thing that finally tips the scales. We study weather and stream flows the way others study the stock market and can get just as cynical about it. On rivers with controlled flows, we imagine that the water board is plotting against us. And a friend from the Midwest says his local weatherman "couldn't predict a fart at a bean-eating contest."

So when the weather abruptly turned skanky, with a low scudding overcast, fitful breeze, and fine, dry snow, I naturally dropped everything and ran up to the river. Sure enough, when I got there I found rafts of flies on the water—slow to get airborne because of the wind and cold—and trout feeding on them in the confident, unhurried way of fish that had finally gotten what they'd been waiting for so patiently. It was the perfect setup, except that the warm days had stretched on for so long that I'd started to think winter would never come, so that when it did, my go bag was still packed for summer. It was a day for a wool sweater, down jacket, fingerless gloves, and a hat with ear flaps, but all I had was a light fleece vest.

I knew I was sunk the minute I stepped out into the cold breeze and the first snowflakes stung my face like needles, but I rigged up and fished anyway because that's what you do. And I did well, considering that I spent better than half my time on the river sitting in the truck warming up. Fifteen or twenty minutes of wading, casting, and releasing the occasional trout with wet hands would send me back for at least the same amount of time in front of the heater. The same thing happened when it came time to change flies, as it always does. Tying the simple knots has long since been ingrained and you'd think you could do it by sight alone, but no. When you can't feel your fingers, you might as well not even *have* fingers. So I'd sit in the cab with a window cracked open a fraction of an inch and my leader threaded inside, waiting for the feeling in my hands to return. Did I listen to the news to kill time? I don't remember, but probably because that's my usual MO. I got hooked on the news at a tender age—if only to find out why Dad was always so pissed-off—and once you've had a taste, it's a hard habit to break. This is how addictions are innocently passed down from one generation to the next.

Naturally there was that one big trout I couldn't get. It wasn't the fish of a lifetime—maybe 16 inches as opposed to the average of

9 or 10—and it was no great drama. I'd show this fish every new fly change, and while some of the smaller trout would fall for it, this one was as fastidious as a cat and wouldn't budge. The flat gray light kept me from seeing it, but I could guess at its size by the extra bulge of water it moved each time it rose. It was probably a rainbow, because the bigger trout here tend to be 'bows, and it wasn't on a hair trigger as some trout are; it would simply stop rising at my first drift as if it were ignoring a panhandler, only to start feeding again as soon as I moved on. I couldn't help but take this personally.

Did I land enough smaller trout to make up for the one larger fish I couldn't fool? It doesn't work that way and even if it did, it would be impossible to tell. Any kind of realistic scorekeeping in fishing would have to account for too many conflicting variables, like landing any fish at all versus the amateur mistake of being too cold to fish in the first place because you forgot to pack for the weather.

I knew it was over the last time I trudged back to the truck to warm up. The afternoon had turned darker and colder; there were fewer flies on the water, fewer rises, and more snow in the air. The dense, gray ceiling had lowered until it obscured the lip of the canyon and I was fighting back the involuntary shivers that are the first warning signs of hypothermia. The truck was running, the heater was blasting, and the gear was stowed, but I gave myself a few more minutes to admire the weather through slapping windshield wipers.

In the upper Midwest, where I grew up, they used to refer to these big northern fronts as "Canadian crap-hammers," but we didn't have color-coded warnings and advisories then; they'd just say we were in for a big one. The adults felt the same elation as the kids at the prospect of a big arctic show, but theirs was tinged with the usual grown-up apprehensions—maybe the power would go out; maybe the car wouldn't start, and if it did, maybe the roads would be impassable. But it was us kids who were up early glued to the radio hoping to hear that school was closed. There's something equally stupendous about the first winter storm in the mountains. You watch dumbstruck as its gray wall settles in with all the indifference of the laws of physics, and the snug cab of the pickup begins to feel flimsy.

Back at home that day, I repacked the go bag as if my next outing would be ice fishing at the North Pole.

An old friend reminds me that I used to fish in the foulest weather hatless, gloveless, and wearing nothing more than a wool shirt and a Levi's jacket. (Old friends are here to remind us who we used to be.) I was in my mid to late twenties then, but I don't recall now if I thought my metabolism was a blast furnace that would keep me warm or if I was going through the tough-guy period so many young bucks of my generation inflicted on ourselves and was just showing off. But like most of us, I outgrew the whole tough-guy business pretty quickly because no one was impressed; they just thought I was stupid.

It probably all started in childhood, as they say most things do. I once came across what I think is the earliest evidence of me fishing, in an old family photo album. It was a black-and-white snapshot of me at about three feet high, barefoot, and shirtless, with a cane pole in one hand and a tiny black fish that must have been a fingerling bullhead in the other. There was no date on the photo and none of the adults who could have taken it were still alive to ask, but the best guess among my cousins was that it was shot in 1950, when I'd have been four years old. I've been told that I was taught to hold a rod and watch a bobber shortly after World War II, but psychologists say we can't remember much before the age of five and, sure enough, I have no memory of it, so fishing has always seemed like less of a learned skill and more of a preexisting condition.

My earliest actual memories of fishing are vague, but they

all seem to involve eating breakfast in the dark and being on the water before first light, even if the fish wouldn't start biting until nine o'clock. I'd be half-asleep and bleary, but a cup of black, bitter coffee brightened things up and would become yet another heirloom addiction. It all had the moral flavor of the manly suffering in an honorable cause that was portrayed in the he-man movies of the time, and although none of my relatives would have been so dramatic as to say, like the Buddhists, that life is suffering, they all had their own version of "anything worthwhile takes work, and work is hard, so man up."

The men of my generation took that to heart. We spent half our lives trying to learn to be grown-ups—even as ideas about what it meant to be an adult male shifted under our feet—until, well into middle age, many of us still hadn't gotten the hang of it and realized we probably never would. All we knew was that we had left behind a trail of things undone and unsaid because they weren't the kind of things a man would do or say. But at least we finally got smart enough to wear a warm coat on a cold day.

So that's fishing as I came to know it: blue-collar, a little rough-and-tumble, sometimes uncomfortable, lightly seasoned with machismo, and unquestionably worthwhile. But then I once read a story in the *New York Times* lifestyle section that began, "Step aside, goat yoga, the chic way to unwind now is fly-fishing," and went on to describe a sport I didn't recognize, complete with "trendy boutique hotels," "fly-fishing-themed, nine-course tasting menus," and an emphasis on stress management, all with the cushy overtones of the glamorous camping that goes by the unfortunate name of "glamping."

I could say that doesn't describe me or anyone I know and not be wrong, but I've always known there was a ritzy end of the sport and I'd be lying if I didn't admit to dipping my toe in it now and then—usually on someone else's dime. I've been to lodges that had chefs instead of cooks (and where the food was better than the fishing). I've had a guide drive me to a private stream in a golf cart. On a fishing junket to the Colorado River I stayed for a few nights at a Four Seasons hotel and I've been served afternoon tea in china cups with linen napkins on a salmon river in Scotland. I always thought it was harmless, especially in small doses, and it's true that no one really wants to be defined by the lifestyle section anyway, but these things can still leak into the atmosphere and even a few parts per million can be toxic.

That same *Times* story also mentioned a contingent of tweedy, old-guard elitists whose stuck-in-the-mud attitudes needed to be ungraded for the twenty-first century. At first, I thought that must be wrong because the old guard was already aging out of the sport by the 1970s, but of course they were talking about people like me, since one generation's upstarts become a later generation's mossbacks.

I finished the story hoping for two things: one, that these folks live long enough to become stuck in the mud themselves—not to be proven wrong, but just to see how it sneaks up on you—and, two, that there are still trout in the rivers by the time that happens.

I never did get dried out on that March day I fell in the river, but I got the worst of the chill off in the dishearteningly clammy way of a grown man sitting alone wearing wet blue jeans. I did think about going back to try for that rainbow again. Almost an hour had gone by, so he'd either be good and ready to eat again or the moment would have passed for good and there was no way to know except to wade back out there and start casting.

I could imagine the story I'd tell: I spotted a good fish, but he wouldn't eat. Then I fell in the river. I warmed up a little while I waited him out and then finally went back and caught the son of a bitch. It would sound heroic to another fisherman, and of course another fisherman is the only one who'd ever hear about it. I could picture the whole drama unfolding like a storyboard for a movie and continued to picture it even as I put the truck in gear and started for home, looking forward to a hot shower and a dry change of clothes.

16

UNCHARTED WATERS

Having a sense about weather is an old way of locating yourself in the world. Farmers and fishermen have always had it and I think I have a touch of it myself that I picked up from my father, a favorite uncle, and other assorted old-timers. But I'm still not above checking the weather report, either online or on the evening news. The forecast isn't always accurate, especially here in the Rocky Mountains, where weather has always been capricious anyway and where, more recently, global warming has threatened to make the computer models that meteorologists depend on obsolete. Susan, the career journalist I've lived with for more than thirty years, once said,

"I always wanted to be a TV weathergirl because it's steady work, you get to wear nice clothes, and it's the only job in journalism where you don't have to be right."

I drove to the river on an early April day with a storm on the way. I knew that from the website of the National Oceanic and Atmospheric Administration, but I could have guessed from the bite of the breeze on a bright blue spring day at 7,500 feet. The sun felt warm on my shoulders, but the air was bitter and smelled like snow, an aroma that's the exact opposite of warm bread fresh from the oven.

I rigged up on the tailgate of the pickup, walked down to the pool I had in mind, and found someone already fishing there. He was wearing a disposable surgical mask, and although it wasn't the first one I'd seen on a trout stream, I still hadn't gotten used to this dystopian sight and knew I never would.

If you count from the first suspicious cases of pneumonia in Wuhan, China, in late December 2019, we were just over three months into the global COVID-19 outbreak, just over a week into Colorado's stay-at-home order, and everyone was still feeling their way into the new reality of virulence and social distancing. Exceptions to that order included "essential" trips to grocery stores and pharmacies (not to mention liquor stores and pot shops) and for "outdoor recreation within ten miles of home." This river was, in fact, about ten miles as the crow flies from my house, never mind that I had to drive farther than that to get there—up one valley, across a narrow basin, and into the next watershed north.

The seriousness of the pandemic dawned on most of us slowly, but it did eventually dawn and then it was all you ever heard about. A few weeks earlier, before the lockdown, I ran my travel plans past my doctor, hoping for some useful tips. She said that with a deadly airborne virus on the loose, I'd have to be nuts to go to an airport, let alone get on a plane and spend hours breathing the recirculated exhaust of hundreds of strangers. It didn't help that I'm in a high-risk group: in my seventies and with the usual underlying condition. Never mind what; everyone my age has something.

Within a week of that conversation, my entire fishing season was cancelled by mutual consent. Half a dozen sorrowful phone calls and emails pulling the plug on British Columbia, Montana, Labrador, Idaho, Minnesota, and points in between. My world had shrunk to parts of two counties in northern Colorado—not the worst place for a trout fisherman to be quarantined, but as spoiled as I've been, it felt claustrophobic.

It didn't help to have politicians and celebrities appearing on TV saying, "We're all in this together," because no one believed it. We understood that those of us who could were getting out to fish from time to time and were otherwise hunkered more or less safely at home, while people making minimum wage were providing us with what we needed, often at great physical risk.

I felt sorry for myself anyway, even though I'm one of the lucky ones. I have good fishing nearby and, as for working from home, I've been doing that for so long I don't know any other way. Many of my friends were in the same boat: freelancers of one kind or another who work at home and are never sure where their next project or paycheck will come from, so over time we've all grown frugal and reclusive. Writers and other such solitary types had it easier than most. You want us to stay home indefinitely with few errands to run and no visitors? Okay. William Shakespeare wrote *King Lear, Macbeth,* and *Antony and Cleopatra* during outbreaks of plague in the 1600s; I should be able to bang out a few fishing stories.

Or, as one friend put it, "Finally I have skills that are relevant." I hadn't heard from this guy in six months and he informed me that he was currently "holed up in New Mexico with a new girlfriend," a situation he described as "interesting." However that works out, it'll go in the books as one hell of a first date.

I walked upstream past the man in the mask—who happened to be playing a trout and was probably smiling, but who could tell?— found the next run vacant, and got in there. It was still two weeks before the average starting date for the Olive mayfly hatch, but it's always been hard for me to locate the actual beginnings of these things. Nothing about fishing is cut-and-dried, and although I have only the sketchiest idea of what goes on in the depths of streams, I do know that weeks before anything a fisherman would describe as a hatch begins, the nymphs must be starting to percolate down there on the streambed, because the trout know what they are and they'll eat 'em when they see 'em. Likewise, once a hatch has petered out, there will be an indeterminate number of days when the odd trout will still eat the fly the way someone always eats the last french fry on the plate. One of the joys of living close to your fishing is that if you put in the time, you can see the whole narrative arc of a hatch: acts one, two, and three and all the way to the final curtain, which in a tailwater like this usually comes abruptly when the water board blows the river up with the first irrigation calls.

I couldn't spot any flies on the water, but the river was still low and clear and I could see a few fish suspended in the current, feeding close enough to the surface to be easily seen, and a few others flashing faintly in deeper water, all presumably eating nymphs. This was still early in the season and I'd been out only a few times. I didn't have my river legs back yet, so I was still wading like a suspect failing a sobriety test and was having trouble tying the knots that would come together so smoothly in a few more weeks. It's not that I had forgotten how to tie knots, but that the signals from brain to fingers were getting lost in translation. I like fishing alone anyway, but I make a point of it early on so no one I know sees me out there fumbling around like a beginner.

Eventually I got a small dry fly tied on with an even smaller soft hackle behind it on an 18-inch dropper. I knew I was pushing my luck—a brace of nymphs with weight on the leader might have been a safer bet—but it's hard not to go right to the rig that's been the hot hand in so many past years. The little soft hackle turned out to be close enough to tempt me to keep fishing it for a while, but still somewhere short of what the fish were actually looking for. I got one small rainbow right off the bat, but then several other fish flashed the dropper without eating, so I finally clipped it off and replaced it with a more conventional mayfly nymph pattern.

That did it. I got three or four more trout on the new dropper and missed a couple of others before a small rainbow ate the dry fly. I took that to mean that even this early a few winged flies were already emerging, although it could have just been one of those eager young trout who will eat anything.

Each time I set the hook and came tight, I'd give the fish its head for a few seconds to see how heavy it was. This isn't known as a big fish river—you'll usually catch chunky rainbows and browns in the 10- to 12-inch range—but every once in a while someone hangs a bruiser and farms it out because they weren't ready.

There were lots of people out that day, which wasn't surprising. Everything nonessential was closed, so many people were either furloughed or outright unemployed. They were bored, unsure of their finances and futures, and had nothing to do except worry or go fishing. For that matter, some who were lucky enough to still be working remotely from home were also sneaking out to the river for a few hours. That's exactly what their suspicious bosses suspected they were doing—going trout fishing instead of staying home to work on the Harris account—while the employees themselves might have said, "What's the difference as long as the work gets done?"

It wasn't just here. A friend from Minnesota said they had already sold a record number of fishing licenses there and he was dreading the walleye opener. Those who think of fishing as a solitary sport have never seen a traffic jam at a boat ramp.

I spent the afternoon on whatever unoccupied runs I could find. Most spots had already been fished through by someone else at least once that day, but when they're on the feed, trout will get back to business pretty quickly after they've been disturbed. Fifteen or twenty minutes is usually all it takes and there are worse ways to spend an afternoon than sitting on the bank of a trout stream, waiting for the fish to start feeding again. On the drive home I was happy I'd caught some fish, but although that morning I thought I was getting out too early, by afternoon I realized I should have been up there a week ago.

The next morning the thermometer read in the low 20s and there was a foot of snow on the ground. It was a shock, even though April and even May snows aren't uncommon here and I knew this one was coming. But true to form for these late storms, a chilly sun had peeked out by afternoon, the snow had already begun to melt into mud, and it was all but gone by the time I made it back up to the river. I picked the next cloudy day because that's what these mayflies like, and I knew I'd hit it right before I even stepped into the water because of the Audubon's warblers. I never see these little bug-eating migrators until the Olive hatch starts, and then overnight the bushes are full of them.

You go to crowded rivers resolved to take whatever you can get, but this time a favorite run was unexpectedly open, so I ducked into the little pullout along the canyon road, locking up a little and spraying some gravel. This is a series of small, braided pools separated by short riffles and culminating at a long, smooth glide known as the Aquarium Pool because it's full of fish and in the right light you can stand on the south bank and count them.

Mayflies weren't exactly pouring off the water, but there were enough around for the fish to get on them, and I hooked trout here and there for the next couple of hours. Most still wanted the nymph dropper, but a few came right to the surface for the dry fly, especially when I could manage to give it the slightest upstream twitch as it entered a trout's line of sight. It's tricky to get this right and it's an easy maneuver to overdo, but if you can pull it off, it sometimes triggers a predatory reflex in fish that have already let a couple of dead drifts go by.

For the longest time I believed that I came up with this tactic on my own—and in fact I did—but it turns out it's no secret. Leonard Wright wrote about it in the 1970s and even gave that little upstream twitch a name. He called it "the sudden inch" even though he admitted that an inch is usually too much. Whenever you think you've discovered something new about fishing, it's only a matter of time before you bump into someone who's known about it longer and does it better.

I even got a couple of fish in the Aquarium, which is famously difficult because the trout have so much time to inspect a fly in the slow currents, but I didn't get the big one. It was a brown trout that rose up beneath my fly, changed his mind at the last second, and sank from sight again, leaving me with just the slow wink of a wide, buttery slab. I gave him two more drifts, then rested him for ten minutes and came back with two similar, but different flies, but no dice. He had nearly succumbed to a moment of weakness, but it seemed clear he wasn't about to make that mistake again.

On my way back to where I'd parked the truck, I spotted two nice rainbows tucked behind a logjam. They were holding in a quick little eddy on the far side of a riffle and they were feeding steadily just under the surface. It was a tricky cast and drift, but I figured if I could wade far enough into the riffle for my line to clear the fast water, I could manage it. If I hooked one it would bolt for the logs, so I'd have to strike sideways and keep the pressure up through the first run. I had it all worked out and got into casting position without spooking them, but when I raised my rod to cast, both fish vanished. It's not that they flushed for cover, but more like they just dissolved in the current without otherwise moving. There one second and gone the next, as if they'd never existed.

Fair enough. Not only can you not catch 'em all, you shouldn't even want to.

It went on like that in fits and starts for the next month. I took to haunting the river on days when the weather was right and sometimes when it wasn't if the sunny days stretched on for too long. On those clear, cool spring days the Colorado sky turns a bottomless blue that I've never seen anywhere else and the light makes every pebble, twig, and pine needle stand out in stark relief. I hate to turn up my nose at such beautiful weather, but it makes for poor dry fly fishing. Then again, the grown men I fished with as a kid would have griped about it, too. I've talked to dozens of women who were horrified at the idea of becoming their mothers, but most of the men I know who have become their fathers seem okay with it.

When the sun was out I'd sometimes stubbornly tie on a dry fly anyway and wander around looking for the odd rising trout. Sometimes I'd find one lurking along a shady bank or under an overhanging bush, but on days when I didn't, I'd give in and fish nymphs for a while, hoping to pick up a fish or two so I wouldn't have to go home skunked. I tend to avoid nymph fishing because I'm not very good at it, although it's not lost on me that I'm not very good at it because I tend to avoid it.

Sometimes I'd go alone and other times I'd be with friends. Instead of riding up together as we used to, we'd go in separate vehicles to maintain a safe distance and meet on the water. (I'm easy to find; just look for the only pickup on the river with no rod caddy and no tackle company stickers.) It was an uncomfortable tactic that wasted gas and felt weirdly standoffish, but it offered the advantage that we could crowd a pulloff with two or three trucks so no one else could squeeze in, thereby establishing squatter's rights to a stretch of river.

I'd worked out a set of rules for wearing a face mask. I'd usually go without one while I was fishing because, as everyone I know has said, fishermen are all *about* social distancing, but I always had one with me that I could slip on if someone got too close. That almost never happened on the water, but sometimes back at the truck someone would wander over to chat the way fishermen do, stopping a fly rod's length away and raising their voice a little to bridge the distance. Or so you hope. In practice, some took social distancing more seriously than others, and since it could end up being a matter of life and death, it was possible to bristle when some numbskull blundered into your six-foot bubble of personal space.

By then I had no fewer than four masks. Real surgical masks were hard to come by even for those in the medical profession, but everyone I knew who could sew was making them, sometimes for sale in an attempt to salvage a fraction of their lost income and sometimes to give away to neighbors and friends as a public service. One of mine was made from a red bandana; another had cartoon cats on it and so on. Overnight, face masks had become a fashion statement. I knew a woman who already had a whole wardrobe of them to match every outfit, even though she rarely left the house. Just as quickly they became a form of political ID, since lefties usually wore them and right-wingers usually didn't.

In order to dodge the worst crowds, I used to avoid weekends like the plague (sorry, bad word choice), but with so many now out of work and at loose ends, every day might as well have been Saturday, so it no longer mattered. The hatch comes off best on cloudy, drizzly days, so that's usually when I went—and so did everyone else. Sometimes I could grab one of the named pools, but they were often taken, so I'd fish the riffly pocket water runs in between. There weren't as many trout, but they were less wary and easier to catch, and on water I'd fished for years I was gradually uncovering new honey holes. Life had gotten unpleasantly strange, with everyone's livelihood in question, including mine, but for the hours I spent on the water I was happy.

People kept talking about "when this is over" and "as soon as things get back to normal," but I didn't have a lot of faith in that. Some politicians said otherwise, but the epidemiologists who knew what they were talking about said that even if everything went right (and it's rare for everything to go right), it could be eighteen months to two years before a vaccine could be developed and distributed and herd immunity began to kick in. That seemed fast to me; the polio vaccine I got as a kid took thirty years to develop. I tried to be philosophical, although if I had to lose a year or two I'd rather have done it in my twenties or thirties, when I had years to spare. But then you don't get to pick the moment when the shit hits the fan.

Meanwhile, I kept getting emails from people in isolation that began with "Well, not much news here . . ." but there were moments of poetry, too. A friend wrote from North Carolina, "Damn, these are strange and uncharted waters, but then we're all sailors at heart."

17

MY FISH

I've heard people say, "It's so quiet up here," but it's not. One minute
the rushing of this creek is reminiscent of faint music, the next of a
distant cheering crowd, and the next of an overheard conversation
in a foreign but familiar language you can almost understand, like
something half-remembered from childhood. And there's the hissing
of wind through aspen leaves and spruce needles, the chattering of
pine squirrels, the pecking of nuthatches, and, because mountain
roads were often built along watercourses, the occasional congested
burble of a downshifting Harley. But yes; depending on what you're
used to, it could pass for quiet.

This was a late morning in mid-July and the stream was nicely down out of runoff with daytime water temperatures in the 50s, smack in the middle of the trout's comfort zone and just right for a wet-wading fisherman in hot weather. When I stopped at the pullout I wanted, I found a school-bus-sized RV with California plates parked there. Its built-in awning was deployed and a well-dressed, silver-haired couple in early retirement age lounged in lawn chairs in its shade, drinking iced tea from tall glasses and looking like an ad for an upscale retirement home. They gave me a suspicious once-over as I walked toward them, but then I put on my face mask and they put on theirs, so by the time I got there we had reached an understanding.

From ten feet away, I asked if they were planning to fish, because if they were, I'd find another spot. They dismissed the idea as if they thought fishing was some kind of diabolical Easter egg hunt, and went on to explain that they'd driven out here to Colorado because the pandemic was bad at home and they wanted to get away from people. "Good idea," I said, almost adding, "Just try not to breathe on anyone while you're here," but then thinking better of it. As I walked away, they said, "Good luck," and I said, "Yeah, you, too."

Down at the creek, I tied on a size 14 Parachute Adams and a soft hackle dropper: go-to flies for me and good bets for this stream and most others like it. My fly box bears the marks of countless previous attempts at reorganization, aiming at completeness one year and simplicity the next without ever quite achieving either. But lately I've tended back toward the Adams again because fishermen of my post–World War II generation keep returning to this hundred-year-old dry fly as if we were coming home after a long, aimless trip.

I like the white wing on the parachute version of this pattern because it makes the fly easier to see, but even then, on the forested stretches of this creek the dappled high-elevation sunlight produces a chiaroscuro effect worthy of Rembrandt, so when even a highly visible fly drifts from brilliant light into black shadow it can blink out like a lightbulb. In fact, it was on this very stream the previous season that I was forced to admit I needed glasses. I'd come to terms with street signs, menus, and movie subtitles getting fuzzy, but it was a different matter on the water. Fly-fishing is a visual sport, but those visuals are real blink-and-you-missed-it stuff even in the best conditions, so when I started losing sight of my fly on the water, I rushed to an optometrist with the siren blaring to get prescription no-line trifocals. It turns out that I hate wearing glasses—they're always dirty, they fog up, they slip down my nose, and with trifocals, I'm forever bobbing my head like an owl to keep things in focus—but I like being able to see again, so it's a bargain I can live with.

I had come to the creek that day to look for one particular trout, although I vowed not to let the day depend on finding it. I'd briefly hooked and lost this fish two weeks earlier while fishing with my friend Vince. We'd been trading off pool for pool and it was my turn when we came to this fishy-looking tub with a plunge at the head and a deep slot against a boulder on the far bank. I caught a pretty little brook trout from the near side of the pool—the kind of fish this creek typically gives up—and as soon as I got the drift I wanted along the bubbly conveyor belt of current against the boulder, a big brown loomed up from the bottom rubble, tugged on the dropper, and then came off with a ponderous wiggle when I set the hook. Vince, who was standing behind and above me with a clear view, let out with the usual "Oh!" or "Whoa!" or some other exclamation that's not exactly a word.

You're expected to provide an estimate of the size of a big missed fish, but there isn't much to go on and anyone you tell will assume you're exaggerating anyway. For that matter, this isn't big-fish water, so when a better-than-average trout does come along, its size is easy to misjudge in the small scale of a creek where 13 inches looks like 16, 16 looks like 20, and you saw it for only a split second anyway.

I had missed another good fish farther upstream on this same creek just a week earlier. I got a late start that day and my first three choices of spot were already taken by other fishermen, so by the time I found an unoccupied place I liked and got my rod strung up, I'd let myself become impatient.

The second-to-last item on my rigging-up checklist—right before tying on a fly—is to run the tippet between my thumb and forefinger to check for nicks and abrasions, and this time I found a wind knot right in the middle of it. Wind knots are misnamed—they're not caused by wind, but by tailing loops in your cast—and they cause weak spots in the leader that should be dealt with. But this time I thought, *What the hell, I won't hook anything big here anyway,* tied on a fly, and started fishing.

You can see this coming. On the second or third cast to the first pool, I got a take, set the hook, and had a brief impression of more weight than I expected before the leader broke right at the wind knot. I found a place to sit on a convenient rock, not to go quietly to pieces as I once would have, but simply to tie on a fresh leader and fly and wonder why I habitually remake the same classic mistakes again and again. But of course, it's that very repetition that makes them classics, isn't it?

So, when I lost that second nice fish no more than a week later, I worried that I was losing my edge or, worse yet, that my luck had gone sideways—something unaccountable that would either have to be ridden out or broken like a curse. I wondered why I always lose the big ones, and then reminded myself that I don't; I lose plenty of smaller trout, too, and take it in stride. And "lose" isn't even the right word, since I never *had* either fish to lose in the first place. Like all trout that aren't already in your hand, they were never more than possibilities.

Anyway, the big trout wasn't there when I went back; not in the slot along the boulder where he'd been before, or the tail of the pool, or the plunge at the head, or even in the next pool upstream, which wasn't as deep, but was shadier on this bright day. Earlier that season, my friend Mike in Minnesota had written to me about a nice fish he'd spotted, marked, and then gone back to later and caught. He even included a photo. His was a brown trout, too, but I thought the one I'd missed was probably bigger. I had such a vivid mental picture of pulling off the same trick that I felt cheated when it didn't happen. I had planned to tell Vince that I went back and got the big brown we saw, and although it would surely have been smaller than we'd guessed, it still would have been impressive for this creek. I wondered if someone had caught and eaten it. I hoped not, but I've done that myself often enough that if that's what happened, it would be unreasonable of me to disapprove.

One recent day on this creek, I met a local spin fisherman I know in passing. He's one of those guys who make it impossible to do anything quickly in a small town because whenever we bump into each other at the market or the post office we feel obliged to exchange local fish stories, always being carefully vague about exactly where they took place. That's annoying when you have a long list of errands to get to, but at the end of the ritual you've been reminded that there was no reason to be in a hurry in the first place, since in our little universe of discourse, catching trout is the only thing that really matters. I sometimes wonder if we'd see eye to eye on any other subject and he may wonder that, too, because we both avoid those other subjects as scrupulously as we do the locations of our secret spots. What we have couldn't be described as a friendship, but whatever you'd call it, neither of us wants to risk having it go sour.

This time when I asked how he'd been doing, he told me that over the last two and a half years he'd been diagnosed with terminal cancer twice, but that after two grueling courses of chemo he was now in remission again. (I hadn't seen him in a while and he did look thinner. His waders that once fit now seemed to be a size too big.) But now, he said, he was trying to regain the thirty-five pounds he'd lost and to that end he had a couple of fat browns on a stringer that he planned to fry up for dinner and the way he described the menu made it obvious that he had regained his appetite. I said, "Good for you," and meant it, but couldn't help noticing that neither of his trout looked big enough to be my fish.

Listen to me: "*my* fish," but that's how I'd come to think of it.

This creek rises in snowfields above tree line on the Front Range, gathers itself in basins in the neighborhood of 11,000 feet, and flows downhill, picking up seeps and a smaller fork until together they join a third creek flowing in from the north to form the main branch of a small river. If you can visualize a creek that drops 5,600 feet down the east slope of the Rockies in no more than forty stream-miles, pooling and falling in response to the topography, you'll have a fair picture of it. This is textbook pocket water: sometimes open and rocky, other times thickly wooded, with stair-step plunge pools, short glides, sudden holes, and steep-sided, boulder-strewn narrows that are almost impassable in places, followed by long, shallow riffles that are unproductive for fishing but produce dissolved oxygen and aquatic insects for the trout in the pools below. Lots of dippers live here, fat, drab little songbirds that dive for the same nymphs the trout eat. In the spring, they sing disconcertingly beautiful songs and build covered nests of dried moss in the rocks that look like brown igloos.

Above the roadside stretch are a few miles that roughly parallel an old logging track that's now only passable in four-wheel drive, and above that is a roadless stretch in a wilderness area where what's left of the old road has devolved into a foot trail that is still haunted in places by the ghosts of twin wheel ruts.

The most obvious remnants of the logging camps are huge piles of slash left from squaring off the logs before they were sawn into boards, but there are also the pilings of a bridge that has since fallen into the creek and washed away, huge old saw blades and other assorted rusting machine parts, and, squatting incongruously at the edge of a pretty meadow like a petrified gnome, a cast iron woodstove where a cook tent must have once stood.

When I moved up here in the mid-1970s, some of the old men who worked these camps were still around and they must have been proud, as old men often are, of the hard, honest work they once did. I came to know some of them in the casual way that I now know that spin fisherman and knew the sons and daughters of a few others. I kick myself now for not prying their stories out of them before they all died out, taking their memories of the old-growth Engelmann spruce and subalpine fir with them. Gary Snyder said, "Much of the work men once did together no longer seems quite right," but that doesn't mean you shouldn't remember when it *did* seem right.

Sometimes in midsummer when the weather is hot and the flows are down, it's worth getting on the water early, but for the most part it's not until late morning or early afternoon that the water warms enough to get things going. This makes for a lazy contrast to childhood memories of being rousted for fishing before daylight at an age when I could sleep till noon given half a chance. Or, later, of those commando types that fly-fishing sometimes produces who say they'll pick you up at six, only to arrive at five fifteen demanding to know if you're gonna lollygag around all day or go fishing.

This creek has always had an indifferent fishing reputation, but people have fished it anyway. It's been the hometown creek for kids and retirees since the 1880s and it will reward patience and sustained attention, although not enough for those who expect more in the way of bragging rights from their sporting lives. Maybe it was once better than it is now, as old-timers have always claimed, or maybe that's just the sentimental memory that erases slow days and combines the good ones into a nonstop massacre of fish.

The place is a case study in microhabitats. Ten feet from the creek, the forest floor of dead leaves and pine duff is dry enough to crunch underfoot, but the humid shade along the water is lush with ferns and patches of moss as perfect as putting greens. They have common names like "grooved gnome-cap" and "hairy screw," but I can't tell one from another. I think of myself as an amateur naturalist, but I'm weak on wildflowers and draw the line at moss identification.

There are fishy lies here that are practically unfishable. Some strain themselves impossibly through sweepers while others are tucked under overhanging branches and can't be reached except with a bow-and-arrow cast. That's where you pinch the fly between thumb and forefinger, draw it back tight against the bend of the rod, and fire it to the target. I know people who are good at this, but for me a successful bow-and-arrow cast is one that doesn't sink the hook point in my thumb.

Even on days when I cherry-pick the easy water, I lose lots of flies here, usually to missed sets that I'll invariably put twenty feet up in a tree. If it's a brittle aspen, I might stand a chance of snapping off the offending twig, but the wiry, bottle-brush clusters of spruce needles grab flies in a hopeless grip and won't let go no matter what. I don't even try anymore; I just break them off and tie on fresh ones. I've accepted lost flies as an unavoidable hazard of the game the way management once accepted concussions in football.

Most days you'll work for your fish here, but a time or two each season everything mysteriously falls together. Fat, hungry trout are everywhere, and if you have any chops at all you'll clean up. (Where have all these gullible fish been up until now? They were here all along, of course. Where else would they have been?) If this happens on a day when you're alone, you'll think twice about telling anyone. Maybe you just say you had a good day and leave it at that, or maybe you play it for laughs like a crazy uncle, claiming the fishing was so good you had to hide behind a tree to tie on a fly. The real story becomes a private matter because not even your friends will buy a glorious day that happened without a witness present.

In the nearly fifty years I've fished here, I've caught a small handful of big trout. Big for a small stream, that is: 16, 17, maybe 18 inches. One came from a deep, mysterious pool far up the drainage where it's rare to see another fisherman. The rest turned up here and there, in ordinary-looking water, at various times of year, and were a complete surprise. Memory isn't always dependable, but it seemed like it had been quite a while since the last one. That's why it was good to break one off—wind knot notwithstanding—and miss another that was big enough to make my partner shout, even if I missed the strike.

I went back to that pullout one last time, in September. The pandemic had become a persistent fact of life by then and I half-expected the Californians still to be camped there, going native. I imagined them with an iron grate over a fire pit and a clothesline strung between trees; the man unshaven, his wife wearing overalls, and both of their fashionable haircuts grown out shaggy. Maybe they had even taken up fishing and I'd find them grilling trout for lunch. But apparently they had moved on, still looking for a good place to get away from people. By that point we had a tanking economy and civil unrest, coronavirus cases all over the country were spiking again after leveling off through the summer, and the West was burning up with wildfires, filling the sky with smoke from the Rockies upwind to

California, where the air quality was said to worse than in Beijing. Not to mention that we were five weeks out from an election so chaotic it made the oldest continuous democracy in the world look like a banana republic. Two thousand twenty had been the weirdest year I could remember—and at my age I can remember some weird ones. In socially distanced conversations with friends, we were all afraid to ask what else could go wrong.

I couldn't shake the sense that my ordinary little days of fishing were being steamrolled by history, but I didn't want to let the season expire without going back one more time to see if my fish was there. I understood that second chances are rare and third chances are all but unheard-of, and it had been long enough now that I'd begun to wonder if all Vince and I had really seen was just a 10-inch trout and a trick of the light.

So, I didn't really expect him to be there and, sure enough, he wasn't, but I caught some other trout that were entirely satisfactory— smaller browns and brookies in their best fall colors—while the sun turned orange in the smoky sky as if evening had arrived hours ahead of schedule.

18

A DAY'S DRIVE FROM HOME

Sometimes the things we muse about actually come true, but with a *Twilight Zone* twist that calls our bluff. I had recently declared in front of witnesses that if I didn't write about fishing for a living, I wouldn't be able to take the kind of trips I do, but that, living here in the northern Colorado foothills, I could fish happily in the streams and rivers within a day's drive from home. Then the coronavirus pandemic hit, destination travel became untenable, and I *could* only fish in the streams and rivers within a day's drive from home.

I wasn't surprised by the unforgiving seasonality of our local drainages—I've lived with that for most of my adult life—but this all hit the fan just as runoff was starting, so it did strike home that fishermen travel for the same reason birds migrate: because when things aren't right here, they're right somewhere else. The only trick is getting there.

With all the local streams running high, Vince and I drove the three and a half hours to a trout lake we like. It's not all that far away in a straight line, but there's no direct route. First you meander north for a while on two-lane blacktops, then turn west up a long river valley, then on north again down a rutted dirt road to where the lake sits in the drainage of another river, this one with its headwaters in Colorado and its mouth in Wyoming.

Any other time, Vince and I would have been riding together and chattering like monkeys, but now we were each driving our own pickups in order to maintain the prescribed social distance. We've traveled and fished together for years and probably haven't exchanged an original thought in a decade, but I missed those inane but still somehow fascinating conversations between fishermen wasting time on the road.

This was a transitional season when we could expect anything at the lake, from size 14 midges to slightly smaller Callibaetis mayflies to migrating damselfly nymphs. The water temperature would be right because the lake is fed by underwater spring seeps and drained by a trickling outlet choked with duckweed. Also, we thought the slow-moving low-pressure front we'd seen on the radar map would give us cloudy skies and no more than a drizzle of rain to make for good fishing weather. It was the usual informed guess that's still just a guess.

At the lake, we got out and stood to stretch, unfolding from our pickups after the long drive like rusty jackknives. The air was cool edging toward chilly, the sky was densely overcast, and the lake was calm but punctuated by passing wind riffles that marked the surface here and there like mackerel clouds. There weren't many bugs on the water, but there were, in fact, some big midges that looked like miniature crane flies, a few Callibaetis duns floating as sedately as sailboats at anchor, and even the odd adult damselfly hovering over the surface, all in insufficient numbers to be called a hatch. But still, a few trout rose sporadically. Most left businesslike dimples and swirls, while one or two others made the splashes characteristic of fish chasing damsels. We hadn't exactly walked into the main event, but it looked promising.

We spread out around the outlet end of the small lake, each finding spots that allowed for a decent back cast through the bankside willows. There weren't enough rising trout to lead any one fish, so I decided to cover water with a brace of nymphs—a damsel with a Callibaetis dropper—casting in a fan pattern and making slow, hand-twist retrieves. Vince probably told me later what fly he was using—it's the kind of thing you always ask—but I don't remember what he said.

We fished for about an hour, during which Vince landed and released a heavy rainbow about 17 inches long and I missed a strike. By "missed" I mean I felt the pull, tightened up, and had the fish on just long enough to feel the elation of hooking one and eagerness for the little drama to come before the line went slack and my thoughts turned to how unfair life can be. And then, because as a fisherman I have tremendous affection and sympathy for trout, I thought, *Okay then, good for you. Next time, be more careful.* An entire emotional roller-coaster ride crammed into the space of three seconds.

Not long after that it began to rain and the restless breeze of an hour ago had become a steady wind out of the northeast—still good fishing weather, except that the wind played hell with the accuracy of my cast. Minutes later, though, the windspeed picked up, the temperature dropped no less than ten degrees, and the rain began to come in gray sheets, seemingly with no air between the drops. When

I saw Vince wade out of the lake and head for the parked trucks, I thought that looked like a good idea. We settled into the cabs of our respective vehicles to wait out what we agreed was just a squall.

I ate my sandwich and a granola bar. I stared out the window for a while. I tried the coffee in my thermos. It was the temperature of old dishwater, but I drank some anyway. I stared out the window again. Then I tried to take a nap, but I wasn't sleepy. Then I was back to staring out the window, cursing myself for not bringing a book. I thought about finally starting on my great American novel (the opening scene would involve a fisherman sitting in his pickup in the rain, staring out the window) but I didn't have either a notebook or a second sentence.

I glanced over at Vince, who seemed to be fooling with his radio. He was looking for the classic rock he's always listening to—the Rolling Stones, the Who—but reception is poor up there and I knew from experience that all he was pulling in through the wall of static was country-western, hog futures, and a guy talking about Jesus.

I rolled down the window to test the air and could see my breath. I rolled the window back up and studied the rain pounding the windshield. It had gained substance now and was closer to sleet or slush or soft graupel. Ice, in other words, which meant that soon the lake would be chilled enough to put the bugs and the fish off at least until tomorrow. This was the kind of weather that could have made for a comfortably lazy day to spend anywhere but in a parked car.

I can't say how much time passed and I may have gone into a bit of a trance, but I glanced over at Vince again when he honked to get my attention. He pointed toward the sky, gave me a theatrical shrug, and then pointed back in the direction we'd come. I nodded and followed him out, hanging back to avoid the rooster tail of mud he threw up behind him. This, then, is a day of spring fishing: a round-trip of seven hours, one hour of casting, a single fish, and no regrets.

We had a slightly higher than normal snowpack that year, followed by spring rains and a big, fat runoff that didn't last long but for the moment had all the local freestone creeks running out of their banks. The only stream that stayed low enough to fish was our nearby tailwater and I spent some time there along with every other fly caster in the county, as well as a whole new crop of beginners; folks who'd been idled by the pandemic shutdown and were looking for a safe and wholesome pastime. (While fishing lodges were closing for lack of customers, hometown fly shops were cleaning up on new gear and socially distanced casting classes.) I guessed that, as with previous booms in the sport, some new recruits would stick with it, while the majority would end up stocking the flea markets of the future with used fishing tackle. In the meantime, they were taking up space, but otherwise not doing much harm.

A few weeks later I went up to the first river Vince and I had driven along on our way to the lake. It had been a death trap for kayakers then, but now that the water was dropping, its pools and riffles were beginning to show and all the driftwood was rearranged like lawn furniture on its freshly washed cobble banks. Tall spruce trees leaning toward the water, glimpses of snowcapped peaks in the near distance, fresh moose poop on the trails, all under that crazy high-elevation light. It's a medium-sized freestone with headwaters in the Never Summer Mountains that I'll never fully understand, but have always liked.

All I had in mind here was to pass some time until the creeks closer to home cleared, but the fishing was good enough that I got pretty involved and ended up going back several times. I had fallen into a kind of pandemic funk. I had plenty of work to do that I wasn't doing and people to see that I wasn't seeing. On the other hand, I'd developed a strong work ethic when it came to trout fishing.

Since I was up there anyway, I finally stopped to photograph some of the old establishments along the river, something that had been in the back of my mind for the last few seasons but that I hadn't gotten around to. These are mid-twentieth-century tourist traps that are long since abandoned and, if not exactly falling down, then are at least ripe for bulldozers making room for God knows what or for going up in one of the wildfires that are increasingly common in the West. The old Kinikinik Store seems especially flammable. It was built in the 1920s of local lodgepole pine logs and has been derelict for so long that this quaint old place now looks like nothing so much as a neat pile of kindling.

Farther downstream there's the sign for the old Rustic Resort, once brilliantly painted, but now faded from years in the sun. It consists of a big red arrow superimposed on a ten-foot-high diving rainbow trout with a line of lightbulbs running along it, many of them now broken. Did the bulbs once cycle on, one after another, in the direction of the arrow in the style of 1950s-vintage diners and used car lots? I assume so, although I never saw the thing lit up.

There's the abandoned Indian Meadows Resort, with its hand-painted sign clumsily depicting a Native American in profile wearing a feathered headdress and smoking a peace pipe. It probably qualifies as folk art as well as the kind of stereotype we once deployed thoughtlessly because, as we now understand, we were thoughtless.

I used my cell phone to take the photos because the phone is a better camera than my camera—a new reality that took a while to sink in. Why bother? I suppose because these places are reminiscent of a time when my parents were alive and young and I was still gullible enough to buy into roadside attractions. On our vacations in the family sedan, we were always game to stop and see the Amazing Reptile Gardens or the World's Largest Prairie Dog, even if the Reptile Gardens turned out to be a couple of rattlesnakes in a box and the World's Largest Prairie Dog was a twelve-foot concrete statue that looked like a brain-damaged gopher. Either we never learned or we found a kind of cosmic humor in the disappointment. We never talked about it because we were the kind of Midwesterners who never talked about anything, so things could go from "Grandpa's feeling under the weather today" to "Grandpa's funeral is next week" without further explanation.

The pandemic meant that I would spend an entire season on my old home water, which is something I hadn't done in years. I was resigned one day and looking forward to it the next, but didn't foresee how nostalgic I'd get. I recalled many of those streams being better decades ago than they are now and sometimes felt as if I'd gone back to visit my favorite college bar, only to find it full of potted ferns and strangers or, worse yet, scrapped for a parking lot.

But then there were enough good days to verify that it's all still there if you know when and where to look. Good fishing is like reading a good, short book: you wish it could last longer, but understand that it's the brevity of it that makes it perfect. So maybe *I'm* the one who's not as good as when I had sharper eyes, better knees, more stamina, and the peculiar enthusiasm of the beginner that, in retrospect, may have made a few hard-won trout seem bigger and more numerous than they really were. When I moved west in my twenties and took up fly-fishing, I had a lot to learn and learned much of it from fishermen who were the age I am now and had the air about them of having been around forever. They seemed so wise at the time, but I've since come to suspect that they had just learned to disguise their bewilderment.

I'm beginning to think now that I may also have had a premonition, because as I write this, on a day in September, there's a wildfire burning up on the river, one of four big ones in the state. The last time I checked, it had grown past 100,000 acres and was 4 percent contained, which is what bureaucrats say when they mean it's totally out of control but they still want to use the word "contained." The most recent Forest Service incident map shows it burning right up to the south bank of the river and all those old abandoned places are on the north bank, but only just, and this is the kind of crown fire that shoots embers out in front of it like artillery shells.

These big, late-season fires don't usually die down until the first good October snows—the same snows that often accompany the Blue-wing Olive hatch—and once that happens the canyon road will reopen and I can get back up there.

I'll have a look at the damage—telling myself it's not disaster tourism because I have a vested interest—then see about the hatch, and, if the fishing is any good, maybe I'll keep a few trout. That had occurred to me the last time I fished there, but, as often happens now, not until I was on my way home with the waders off and the rod broken down. It was akin to the feeling you get when you're halfway home from the store and remember you forgot to get milk, so, as regrets go, it was the kind of small one that's easy to live with.

19

EVERY POSSIBLE WAY

For most of the twenty-three summers I've lived in this house, a pair of small flycatchers called western wood-pewees have built a nest right outside my office door, in a notch on the exterior wall that looks like it was once intended to anchor a beam. Every time I open that door, I flush a bird off the nest, so as soon as I notice the activity, I make a point of walking upstairs to go out through the kitchen. At first I'll lock that door as a reminder, but after a week or so the detour becomes second nature.

I think of these as the same birds year after year, but this has been going on longer than any bird's life span, so they can't be.

Maybe they're the descendants of some original pair returning to the old family nest site, or maybe it's just an ideal spot: out of the wind, sheltered from weather, and too high up a wall for predators to climb. These are nervous, olive-colored, sparrow-sized birds with the reaction times of fighter pilots, uniquely adapted to catch flying insects out of the air and endlessly fascinating to watch. I could claim they're a distraction, but window-gazing figures prominently in my work routine anyway, so it's not their fault.

The nest was complete and the female was brooding her clutch of eggs when the runoff in the local streams began to wane in the last week of June. That's early as runoffs go, and I have a good feel for it, having seen fifty-one consecutive spring floods here on the east slope of the Colorado Rockies. The streams were still running high, but they had cleared and dropped just enough that some of the pools had begun to regain their shapes, and since I'd hardly been out in a month, I convinced myself they were fishable.

But they really weren't. Some runs looked good from a distance, but when I got down there and made a cast, the fly would rip through, towing a wake. Or if an eddying current *was* slow enough for a good drift, it was out of reach across a creek that was still too high and fast to cross, leaving me to wonder, for the hundredth time, why the best-looking spots are always on the wrong side of the river. Now and then I'd manage to hook a trout, but as the old joke goes, if it always worked, they'd call it "catching" instead of "fishing."

The four to six weeks of runoff are when I usually blow town looking for better conditions elsewhere, but that was out of the question this year. The coronavirus was out of control, and destination travel, with its airplanes, hotels, and unavoidable crowds, was too risky. The border with Canada was closed and I couldn't blame Canada. Americans already had a reputation for being bat-shit crazy and heavily armed and now we were contagious, too. It didn't matter anyway because many of the lodges and outfitters had shut down for lack of customers. Back in America, some states wouldn't even sell you a nonresident fishing license, while others would but insisted that you quarantine for fourteen days before hitting the rivers. There was no way around it; it was home water or nothing, and for more than a month it had been next to nothing.

I drive along the North Fork of our local river on my way into town and I didn't even have to look at the water to know it was still in runoff; I could tell by the platoons of tubers deploying at the two bridges. I recognized a few as locals, but most had driven over from neighboring towns because up here the river is steep enough to make tubing a proper thrill ride. I always thought of this as harmless fun if only because when the river is best for tubing, it's largely unfishable, but here they were again in the midst of a global pandemic: young and oblivious, with no face coverings or attempts at keeping their distance. As I'd drive by with my responsible adult face mask and hand sanitizer on the seat next to me, all I could see was a Petri dish of contagion that made me feel righteously aloof one day and just grumpy the next, although an especially fetching bikini could lighten the mood.

That's how things stood when a veterinarian friend invited a couple of us over to fish the stretch of stream that runs through his property. The water was still high, but this was lower down where the river leaves the canyon and flows though a milder landscape called Apple Valley. There it widens and slows enough to be almost fishable.

At the downstream end of the property there were two good back-to-back runs that were still ripping right along but had softer slicks on the insides that looked promising with a dry and dropper. The trout we got there were chunky little wild browns—the de-scendants of fish stocked generations ago—and they were as fat and innocent as trout get after feasting undisturbed in high water. Even the smaller ones jumped when they were hooked, and if they got into the fast current, they'd take a few turns of line off the reel.

At the top of the second run, where the river makes an eastward turn, we found a fully inflated beachball caught in the bankside willows. I'm always appalled by the preposterous junk that washes up in rivers and my first impulse was to puncture it with my pocketknife and dispose of it. But it still looked bright and new enough to have been lost earlier that same day and my friend Doug suggested that we toss it back into the current so it would float down to the park in town, where some kid would find it. A much more generous suggestion.

Upstream, closer to the owner's house, there are some pools that have been stocked with rainbows. This is a thing you do when you own a stretch of river: dump in more and larger trout than would normally live there and then, whether you'd planned on it or not, end up doing some supplemental feeding because there isn't enough natural forage to support them. Once word gets out (and word always gets out), the local trout bums begin to haunt the borders of the property, knowing that big trout sometimes get restless and go looking for better accommodations, and some of the bolder fishermen can't help nipping around the edges a little, no-trespassing signs notwithstanding. Anyone who aspires to own a stretch of trout stream should spend an hour listening to the concerns of someone who already does.

It was in one of those pools that I hooked what looked and felt like a 5-pound trout. The current here was fast and loud, but there was a placid slick along the far bank where I could manage a short, drag-free float by perching on a rock and throwing a high-stick cast with a hard, upstream mend. I was watching the dry fly the way you'd watch a bobber above a worm when it went down in a softball-sized bulge and I set up on more trout than I'm used to.

I had him on a 4-weight bamboo rod that was too light for his size and he could have easily gone over the lip of the pool into the riffle below to make his escape, but he chose not to, and that gave me my break. I let the fish have line as he made his short, determined runs around the pool and then gained it back when he let up, following John Casey's simple rule: "When the fish does something, you do nothing, and when the fish does nothing, you do something." The fish had rolled at the surface once and revealed himself to be a rainbow noticeably over 20 inches long and thick in the body. I was beginning to make headway toward wearing him down when a pair of tubers came around the bend on their way through the pool.

I just looked up and they were there, and judging by their expressions, they'd have said the same about me. We were each the last thing the others expected to see. At about the moment I saw these two, the guy in front took in what was happening and tried to pull off an emergency dismount, but he was too close and the current was too fast, so all he managed to do was flounder into the pool, making more of a commotion than if he had just floated on through, and causing the fish to bolt and break off. I stood there with a slack line as the second guy bobbed by like a piece of driftwood, giving me a sheepish grin and a shrug. I thought I'd lost big trout in every possible way, but this was a new one. I glanced over at Doug. He was doing his best to put on a sympathetic expression while trying not to laugh.

I'll admit that for an instant my heart filled with murderous ha-tred for these tubers as well as every last one of their fun-hog col-leagues with their stupid beach toys. I tried to tell myself this had only been a pampered stocked fish instead of a real, wild trout, but there's an acquisitiveness that kicks in when you hang a big one that won't listen to reason. In the end, though, I had to shrug it off. After all, the guy had seen too late that he was about to barge in and ruin everything, tried to pull off the last-minute save anyway, only making things worse—and who among us hasn't done something like that?

It was late afternoon by then and a thunderstorm was building up the valley, complete with slate-colored clouds, a chilly breeze, and strobes of lightning that seemed unconnected to the guttural rumbles that arrived seconds later. The air had gone out of another day of fishing and it was time to go home and let the little tragedies of sport take a back seat to the promise of leftover meat loaf. Doug and I agreed to wangle another invitation later on when the river dropped enough to fish well and the tubers were gone, as they eventually would be. As persistent as some of them are, sooner or later the flow would get so low they'd be bruising their butts in the riffles and even the die-hards would pack it in.

We had come into that spring with a slightly higher than average snowpack, but summer shaped up hot and arid, the monsoon rains were disappointing, and the streams dropped quickly until by late July much of the West was in a drought. Still, for a while the fishing was more or less normal, except that so many people had time on their hands because of the pandemic that the state had sold 90,000 more resident fishing licenses than they had the year before. Think about that number for a minute. Now try to imagine them all stomping around in your home water, where you used to go for peace, quiet, and a few trout. To avoid all those people, my friends and I took to sniffing out the most obscure and difficult stretches of our local creeks, and after years of fishing here we at least had the advantage of knowing where those places are. Most days the fishing was anywhere from okay to downright good, and although I'd now and then wonder if I was getting too old for all this bushwhacking and rock scrambling, there I was doing it, so apparently not.

Wildfire season began in midsummer, as always, but the combination of drought and global warming made it a bad one. By

September there were four big fires in Colorado, plus dozens of smaller ones and more than a hundred more upwind all the way to the Pacific. The sky was gray with smoke and the collective plume eventually reached all the way to the West Coast with the prevailing winds and out over the Atlantic. The Weather Channel showed satellite photos of it.

The fires caught up with us in October. We had lived with them for so long that they'd begun to seem almost normal, like a long stretch of miserable weather, but then one day we found ourselves surrounded on three sides, with Cameron Peak (which would become the biggest wildfire in state history) burning ten miles to the north, East Troublesome (destined to be the second biggest) the same distance west, and Calwood four miles to the south.

Overnight, everyone we knew in the area was packing up to evacuate and a few had already left, including our friend with the trout stream. He had rounded up wife, kids, and the odd menagerie that vets always seem to accumulate—everything from dogs to ducks to llamas—and headed to a friend's ranch following the cardinal rule of evacuation: look after everything with a pulse first; the rest you can either replace or live without. He bolted earlier than some because wrangling that many animals isn't a chore you want to leave till the last minute. (Dogs can be whistled up, but have you ever tried to catch a duck?)

I packed my Jeep with fly rods, artwork, and books and parked it at a friend's house a safe distance away. Back home I loaded more stuff in the pickup and assembled the usual stack of important documents you supposedly can't do without. They fit easily in a plastic milk crate with room left over for fly reels and some portable keepsakes like Grandpa's pocket watch and Dad's knife and compass.

At its worst, we could step out on the back porch after dark and see flames on two horizons. There was so much smoke and ash in the air that birds were strangling on it and falling dead from the sky. I found juncos, chickadees, and finches, but no flycatchers. They commute between the Rockies and the Andes, following a constant supply of flying insects through an endless summer, and had long since left. I don't really envy the lives of animals (they're too brief and urgent for my taste) but the idea of being unencumbered and airborne was momentarily attractive. The perfect little bird corpses were always gone the next morning, cleaned up overnight by raccoons or whatever else was sniffing around out there after dark.

I'd largely lost track of fishing for a while, but driving in to check on my friend Vince one day, I couldn't help noticing that the stream running through the vet's land had been depleted by the drought until it wasn't much more than shallow, stagnant pools connected by halfhearted trickles of current: the kind of meager flows that are known to winterkill trout of any size. I found Vince on his ATV checking on the irrigation ditch he manages. He'd been ordered to evacuate but had stayed on to keep the ditch full in case homeowners and firefighters along its course needed the water. He had the tools of the trade with him, including a long-handled pitchfork, and we joked about taking it over to our friend's place to clean the remaining trout of his pools for a fish fry. It was the kind of cruel wisecrack we men come up with in lieu of admitting how we really feel.

We spent some sleepless nights but never did have to evacuate. The high winds that had driven the fires finally brought in cold and snow that made them lie down enough for firefighters to get better containment. A week later there was more snow and even better containment and gradually the evacuation orders that had crept so close were rescinded one by one. Still, it was another week or so before we started unloading the vehicles and bringing things back in the house, careful not to jinx things by seeming too eager.

There are snap decisions to be made when you pack up to

evacuate, followed by a moment when you glance around at the rest of a lifetime's worth of possessions that you won't be able to take with you and wonder, *Is all this stuff who I am, and, if so, who would I be without it?* Later, when the smoke clears and the only damage is to your nerves, the memory of that question makes you more generous to your neighbors who didn't fare so well. Occasionally it's real physical help, but in most cases, it's just money, which won't cure every heartache but can still work wonders in sufficient amounts and conveniently doubles as self-medication for survivor's guilt.

By the time it was all over, in November, the better part of a month was gone, for all practical purposes the fishing was over, and I had missed more of it than I would have liked. It's true that there's always next year, but even a normal fall still seems like the end of something you'll never get back. I tried my best not to complain, because so many others had it so much worse, but in a weak moment I unloaded on a friend from the west slope. She wrote back, "Yes, but in spite of that, beauty is all around us," and I didn't have it in me to say, "No, it isn't."

The week before Thanksgiving, Vince and I drove up to the Cache la Poudre River to look at the aftermath of the Cameron Peak Fire. On incident maps, the borders of burns are drawn as straight lines for convenience, but on-site there are black moonscapes punctuated by ragged islands and peninsulas of green, sometimes surrounding undamaged cabins a stone's throw from rectangular foundations presided over by scorched chimneys. It reminded me of the tornados in the Midwest that could scatter one house across ten acres while leaving the place next door intact. But of course, in this case the firefighters deserved as much credit as the capriciousness of the fires, and they got it in the form of hand-painted signs reading "Thanks Firefighters" or "We love our first responders."

This is a river we like to fish and we had brought our gear just in case, but we never even strung up our rods. For one thing, this all seemed too raw and personal to be gawked at by strangers, so we weren't entirely comfortable even being there. And for another, the temperature was in the 20s, with a stiff breeze and spitting snow. No doubt a few trout could still have been caught, but somehow fishing season already seemed like a memory.

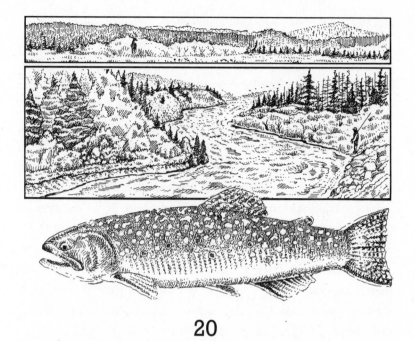

20

ALL THE TIME IN THE WORLD

Vince and I were on the west side of the nearby national park fishing the headwaters of the Colorado River. Each of us had fished over here separately back in the 1970s and '80s and had memories of the place that roughly coincided, not that it would have mattered if they hadn't. Even without global warming and increased fishing pressure, trout streams change over time and so do fishermen, and by then a fair amount of time had passed.

Vince and I lived in and around this county for a long time before we met, so we have an entire catalog of these independent recollections in common: good local rock bands that should have hit it big, but didn't; open meadows where there are now houses; a mom-and-pop café that's long since closed, but where, as younger men, we each swore never to become one of those annoying goobers with a big gut and no ass who like to tease waitresses. (You want a waitress to remember you? Be polite and leave a good tip.) And of course, many trout streams—near and far, good, bad, and indifferent—that may or may not be the same now as they were then.

The majority of this park's four million–plus annual visitors cluster on the east slope, where access is easy. This corridor has gotten so congested in recent years that the park finally resorted to a timed-entry permit system involving schedules and paperwork in an attempt at crowd control. There are some good creeks up there that we used to fish but eventually had to write off as more mobbed than a shopping mall at Christmas and with less parking, while in a masterpiece of marketing, the park continues to publish photos of these spots as pristine wilderness without a human in sight.

This has never been holy ground for fly casters on the order of Yellowstone, but it's still a national park in the Rocky Mountains with snowcapped peaks and trout streams; you can hire guides in the nearby town and the airport in Denver is only sixty miles away by rental car, so it's always been flypaper for tourists. Those of us who live nearby never actually had these streams all to ourselves, but we once knew how to sidestep the crowd by coming earlier, staying later, or walking farther, although it's only in retrospect that we understand how good we had it. It's not that being here early puts us on some moral high ground. It's just that back before we loved the place to death, there really was more room to fish, the trout were bigger, and there were more of them. That's the standard lament, made no less poignant by being true.

The west slope is less crowded partly because to get over there from the east side, you have to cross the Continental Divide by way of Trail Ridge Road, a white-knuckle drive that takes you upward of 12,000 feet on a narrow two-lane that in places has sheer drops, no guardrails, and distracted sightseers straying over the centerline. The National Park Service describes the trip as an adventure from the comfort of your own car, but "comfort" isn't the word I'd use.

You could say I suffer from acrophobia (fear of heights) except that I don't recognize it as a psychological condition, but as a commonsense acknowledgment of the fact that if you fall a great distance, you'll die. I didn't always have it. As a kid, I climbed my share of tall trees and fell out of a few, getting the usual cuts and bruises, but suffering no lasting emotional damage. And later, on a four-thousand-mile road trip in my late teens, I crossed the Mackinac Bridge, which connects Michigan's upper and lower peninsulas. This five-mile-long suspension bridge is so scary that there are people on duty at the toll booths who will drive you across if you can't face it. (It's the see-through, open-grid roadbed that does it for most.) It's not always who you'd think. For every timid tourist in a minivan, there's a burly truck driver or lumberjack who has to relinquish the wheel and ride across cowering in the fetal position, afraid to even look.

I was with a friend the day we crossed that bridge in a 1950s-vintage Volkswagen and I don't remember which of us was driving, but I do recall sailing over the straits between Lakes Michigan and Huron without batting an eye, two kids fresh from high school in the Midwest on our way to Haight-Ashbury in 1964, three years before the Summer of Love, when hippies made the evening news and the utopian dream had already begun to fade.

The first attack I remember came years later when a friend and I hiked to the top of a bare, windy ridge in the Northern Rockies. At the summit I found myself unable to straighten up from a deep crouch, as if I had bent over to pick up a newspaper from the porch and frozen in that position. My friend helpfully said, "You won't bump your head on the sky if you stand up," but I wasn't buying it. The sky seemed way too close and, even bent over like I was, the ground looked too far away. The view from up there must have been breathtaking, but I didn't have breath to spare and couldn't bring myself to look.

That wasn't long after a friend who had been teaching me the fundamentals of ice climbing with crampons, ropes, and ice ax died in a fall from a glacier. They say anyone who psychoanalyzes himself has a fool for a patient, but it's hard not to put a finger on that as the precipitating event. All I really know is that the death of a friend hits you harder when you're young and, up until that moment, still thought of yourself as invincible. My flirtation with mountaineering began to wane on my way home from the funeral, when I vowed to spend less time dangling high above the ground and more time fly-fishing.

I didn't panic up on Trail Ridge and even managed to hold up my end of the conversation as Vince drove us over the pass. I took in the precipitous view—although I didn't enjoy it—and was duly impressed by the sight of hundreds of elk grazing across near-vertical alpine tundra, looking fat and happy in the cool air and warm sun above tree line. But I was relieved to come down into the spruce and fir forest on the west side and loosen my death grip on the armrest, thinking, *God, the things I do for fish.*

It's in the nature of rivers to start small. At its headwaters at Lake Itasca in Minnesota, you can cross the Mississippi on stepping-stones, so it's not surprising to see the Colorado beginning as a narrow creek fed by springs and snowmelt seeps and snaking its way south across Kawuneeche Valley. This is the kind of shaggy, open meadow above 8,000 feet where you might see elk grazing or spot a moose materializing out of the dark timber while cloud shadows wander the valley at a leisurely walking pace.

Returning to a place like this after a long absence sometimes gets you warbling like a lonesome folksinger about how things used to be, but we found the creek to be more or less as we remembered—eminently fishable, but nothing to write home about—although it was skinnier than usual now because of that summer's drought. The east slope of the Continental Divide, where Vince and I live, had been hot that summer and so smoky from wildfires farther west that some days it was like living next door to hell. Due to a trick of the weather patterns, it had been more or less normal in terms of precipitation and stream flows. But as soon as we crossed the Divide going west, we entered the zone shaded yellow on the state drought map for "abnormally dry," and if we had driven on west toward Utah, we would have gone from tan for "moderate," to orange for "severe," and ended up in fire engine red for "extreme," while farther west, in parts of Utah, Nevada, and California, you would enter maroon for "exceptional drought." Of course, things like climate and wildfires ignore state lines as if they didn't exist because they really don't. The Mountain West is a varied but coherent bioregion, while "Colorado" is just an arbitrary square drawn on a map by politicians in the nineteenth century without regard for natural or preexisting cultural boundaries.

It's the same with rivers. The Colorado flows through seven states in the United States and two more in Mexico and it was in better shape here in its headwaters than at its mouth. One thousand four hundred and fifty miles downstream, where it empties into the Sea of Cortez, the river that carved the Grand Canyon regularly runs dry, the victim—even before the droughts—of bad laws that allocate more water rights than there is water, as if no one would ever notice.

We found the same brook trout that we remembered from last time: fish that were first stocked in what was then the Colorado Territory in the early 1870s to replace the native cutthroats that were already getting fished out. Those transplanted Eastern fish took to the cold, clean water at the higher elevations and have hung on in some mountain creeks for a century and a half. In most places they did replace the native fish, which is a damned shame, but then, for some of us at least, they went on to become frontier relics in their own right with the same corny romance as ghost towns, old saddles, and wagon wheels.

Brook trout evolved their prey-species defense mechanism of breeding like rabbits in waters they shared with pike and lake trout, but the habit persists even without those efficient predators to cull their numbers, so that here in the Mountain West they tend to overpopulate and stunt. That's why some fishermen don't like them, although if their average size were closer to 18 inches than to 8 or 9, that prejudice would vanish. It's also why Colorado Parks & Wildlife allows fishermen to keep ten extra brook trout 8 inches long or less in addition to the normal daily bag limit of four. I'm not sure you can reasonably expect fishermen to collectively eat you out of a fisheries management problem, but that's their reasoning and I do my part now and then with brook trout fried in bacon grease along with an appropriately Western side dish like pork and beans or fried potatoes.

We found the fish where you always find them, tucked here and there in the impressive variety of habitat these meadow streams generate with nothing more to work with than gravity and the tendency of current to meander. There are seemingly infinite variations on the theme of one S-curve after another with bend pools, tubs, undercuts, glides, eddies, slots, channels, and brush jams, all separated at odd intervals by pretty sunlit riffles, and no two alike. A good trout stream is like a good paragraph; linear and recognizable, but with a little surprise around every corner.

Fly casting here is more demanding than on bigger water. There's less room for slop, less room for long, stealthy drifts, less room, period. Much of it is recognizable short-range casting, but sooner or later you'll end up high-sticking an improvised cast from a kneeling position in order to get a drift in some miniature but irresistible sweet spot.

Vince and I warmed up as usual by cherry-picking easy spots with casually sloppy casts and then began to bear down as we picked out the less obvious honey holes. I remember a dinner-plate-sized eddy in an undercut bank—deep, shaded, half overhung with grass and cupping a little foamy backwater: just the kind of place a larger than normal brook trout would pick to hide. So I engineered a cast that dropped the fly in the quarter inch of bankside current that would draw it into the eddy for a single slow revolution. I managed to pull off a couple of good ones without getting a grab, but nonetheless a switch had been thrown; I was now taking the creek on its own terms, fishing for its 9-inch brookies as if they each weighed 5 pounds.

This was mid-July, on a high summer day made for wet wading in shorts, but already the male brookies were beginning to ease into their fall spawning colors. Their olive flanks had begun to darken, their yellow vermiculations and blue-haloed red spots had brightened, and their bellies were flushing the rosy pink that by August would become the orange band that flashes in the sun when they roll on a dry fly. Every fisherman's favorite fish is the one he's casting to at the moment, and that day mine were brook trout.

These mountain creeks tend to be ordinary, but because of that they're generous with everything else fishing should offer, but sometimes doesn't: peace and quiet, unobstructed views, eager trout, solitude or company depending on your mood, maybe a hawk wheeling overhead or a raven croaking like a frog with a sore throat, and the kind of easygoing pace engendered by fisheries so far from being world-class that they'll never attract crowds. The only thing they don't have is big fish, and there are still places to find those when the need arises.

Most of my fishing friends have soft spots for small streams, including my late friend Paul, and this was the summer when I had finally begun to think about where to put his ashes. Paul died four years earlier, just a few weeks after Vince and I took him out fishing one last time. (Later in life, the death of a friend is no longer unbelievable because you've learned about mortality the hard way, but that doesn't make the news land any easier.) That day doesn't make for an especially good memory. Paul had been terminally ill for some time by then, so it was no fun watching him struggle to land a few trout and pooch some easy sets because his reflexes were shot. This outing had been Paul's idea, but I wonder now if it wasn't more for our benefit than his—a left-handed way of saying good-bye without coming right out and saying it.

Most of his ashes were scattered where he liked to fish in his native Michigan, but his grown son and daughter thought some should also go here in Colorado, where he came often on summer-long fishing and couch-surfing expeditions. The kids naturally wanted to be here for that, but that first year, time for the trip and money for plane tickets were both scarce, so we put it off. Then the pandemic hit and no one was going anywhere and now that things have begun to open back up, we've all gotten busy again and the urgency has leaked out of the plan like air from a tire. As it stands now, some of Paul's ashes have been here at the house for several years, sitting in a sunny windowsill in a Tupperware tub that has begun to seem like just one more ordinary thing people have around home, like a houseplant on the kitchen table.

Early on there was talk of putting his ashes in the run where he caught his last few trout, but we've since lost access to that stretch of creek when ownership of the land changed hands. If it seemed important, we could ask permission and sneak on anyway if the answer was no, but Paul was the kind of guy the upper Midwest

ALL THE TIME IN THE WORLD

once produced in quantity: a quiet, modest, happily anonymous man who wouldn't be sentimental about where his ashes should go. I can almost hear him shrugging off the whole business with something like, "Anywhere but down the toilet, okay?"

So I had been idly waiting for the right spot on the right creek to jump out at me with the certainty of a revelation, although in the end it may not happen that way. I'm sometimes startled by how mundane a chore this has become, but then Joe Biden said, "The day will come when the memory of the person you lost brings a smile to your lips before it brings a tear to your eye." Maybe that smile is what tells you it's time to finally do something with the ashes and when the time comes, someone should be prepared to say, "I know just the spot." In the meantime, there's no hurry. Like most fishermen, Paul always acted like he had all the time in the world, and now he does.

Vince and I caught our share of fish that day and were back at the pickup a little after two o'clock, as we had planned. In the droughts and heat waves that are becoming the rule rather than the exception in the West, we've learned to get off the water in early afternoon, even at these higher, cooler elevations, to avoid stressing the trout by catching them in water that's gotten too warm. (This is known regionally as "the hoot owl rule," but don't ask me why.) Often enough, the fish make the decision for you by going off the bite on their own, but we keep an eye on the clock anyway. When the time came, Vince led the way across the meadow toward the road, skirting bog holes and beaver channels hidden in the grass, and as he walked ahead, the ice in his half-full metal water bottle tinkled as if he were mixing a martini.

I had to get home early that day anyway to grab a shower, change into clean clothes, and drive Susan and another couple to a restaurant in a nearby town for one of Susan's ongoing series of birthday dinners. Susan was Paul's cousin—which is how he and I met in the first place—and in the years we've lived together, she's never been satisfied with a single birthday per year, but prolongs the festivities by designating all of July as her "birthday month."

So that night we picked up our friends and drove the twenty miles to the restaurant, where we went through the usual pantomime of masking up like a surgical team to walk in and be led to a table on the patio out back, only to take the masks off and fold them on the table next to us like spare napkins. This is a seafood place with fish flown in fresh daily, so I scanned the specials out of habit, but I'd built up a good appetite and already had my heart set on a big plate of creole jambalaya with homemade cornbread—a more than adequate substitute for fried brook trout. Since I quit drinking, I've become everyone's designated driver, so while the others shared a few celebratory bottles of wine, I ordered iced tea and got an approving nod from our waitress. I quit so long ago now that most days I no longer even *want* a drink, but she assumed I was making this brave little sacrifice to keep those close to me safe.

21

WHAT I KNOW NOW

This was my first time on an airplane since the onset of the pandemic and I didn't know what to expect, but at the airport in Denver I found the same crowd of impatient strangers I had waded through over a year ago, except that now everyone was wearing face masks, as per Transportation Security Administration regulations. By then I'd come to hate masks, but also to believe in them as the best shot at protecting me from others and others from me—and my goal from the beginning had been to come through this pandemic alive and with a clear conscience. But some of those others clearly *weren't* happy about it and I could feel the incipient air rage crackling through the place like static electricity. Nonetheless, I was happy to be traveling again and noticed that I wasn't the only one carrying a pack and a rod case. On the way to my gate, I passed a man who said, to no one in particular, "Everybody's goin' fishin'. I freaking love it."

In Bozeman, I found my duffel on the baggage carousel and my friends Dan and Mike waiting outside. Dan had driven out from South Dakota and Mike had come in from Minnesota, each arriving here in white SUVs so similar they could have been part of the same corporate fleet. Plenty of things puzzled me as a kid (puzzlement comes with the territory of childhood) but I was especially impressed by the ability of adults to leave from disparate locations and converge unerringly at a predetermined place and time. I've since grown up and learned the trick, but to this day I'm always a little surprised to see anyone I planned to meet.

Dan had left his young Lab, Leo, at home with his daughter, but Mike brought along his new yellow Lab puppy, Buncie—a family nickname. Buncie is six months old, already forty pounds (Mike likes 'em big), and everything you'd expect from a Labrador pup. He's the most recent in a long line of Labrador retrievers in Mike's life. In the earliest photo I've seen of him with a Lab, Mike is barely taller than the dog.

I was happy to meet Buncie but caught myself missing Mike's old Lab Moose, who was such familiar company on previous fishing trips. Moose is still with us, but he's too old and arthritic now to get around on trout streams, so he now stays home with Mike's wife, Andrea, getting slow walks in the cool mornings and sleeping away the afternoons in the air-conditioned house. Who knows what dogs think, but I imagine that he misses going fishing because I would and the origin of empathy is always the selfish question, What if that were me?

We made the Big Hole River in time to get our nonresident

licenses at the fly shop in Melrose, where our out-of-state plates branded us as tourists, even though Mike grew up here, fishing from childhood through high school and beyond, and probably knows more fishy nooks and crannies of this region than the guides. Then we hit the water for a few hours before dark. Within months the Big Hole and other rivers in Montana would be closed to fishing because of low flows and warm water, but this was the last day in May and the river was just coming into a modest runoff, crowding the bankside willows and running clear, cold, and fishable. We landed only a handful of trout that evening and nothing big, but there was still the satisfaction of buying licenses, driving straight to the river, and catching fish.

Two days later we were back at the shop early for the floats we'd booked: one boat for me and Dan, the other for Mike and Buncie. Mike's guide, Erik, had said on the phone that he was fine having a dog in his boat as long as it was well-behaved. Mike assured him that Buncie was a perfect gentleman but admitted to us later that the dog had never even seen a boat, let alone been in one, so who knew?

When Erik met Buncie that morning, his expression suggested that most dog owners wouldn't know "well-behaved" if it bit 'em in the ass, but it all went fine. Almost every time we saw Mike that day he was playing a fish, while Buncie sat patiently in the bow seat, a portrait of composure. Buncie started going fishing when he was small enough to be tucked into Mike's waders for a nap when he got tired, so even at six months, fishing was entirely familiar to him, even if the boat was a new wrinkle.

The hatch of big salmon flies and the crowds of fishermen they attract weren't due for a few weeks yet, but we knew the nymphs would be active and that the fish would be on them, so we dredged large, dark stone fly nymphs along the banks. Dan's real jones is fly-fishing for carp—he literally wrote the book on it, *The Orvis*

Beginner's Guide to Carp Flies—and ominously claims that they're the fly rod fish of the future, but he's a good enough trout fisherman that he could probably write that book, too.

So Dan caught fish, including some nice ones, and so did I, although we wondered why Mike was doing so much better. We speculated about it idly throughout the day (better flies? better guide?), always carefully avoiding the possibility that he was just a better fisherman with a home court advantage. Mike isn't normally one to show off, but he was having such a good day he couldn't resist pulling off a little stunt for a finale. He hooked a good brown trout sixty yards from the takeout and walked it downstream like a dog on a leash so he could land and release it right in front of us while Buncie disembarked to take a long, luxurious piss on the beach.

We were staying nearby in a spare house on a sheep ranch owned by Mike's high school friend Erik Kalsta—not to be confused with Erik the guide. As generations come and go on these family spreads, they sometimes leave behind unused homes that become guesthouses by default. We woke each morning to robins singing and lambs bleating and were off fishing most days while the bustle of chores went on, but it wasn't lost on us that a sheep ranch in springtime is an idyllic place to stay as long as you don't have to do the work.

Erik would wander over after dinner most evenings and we'd sit on the porch, swatting mosquitoes and talking. Erik is the kind of well-informed, good speaker who's said to be effective at public meetings and has an inside-out knowledge of the place where he's lived all his life—its natural and human history, economics, ranching practices, politics, and regional eccentricities. He's befriended university biologists and monitors game cameras on his property, and although he doesn't fish himself, he knows more about the ecology of rivers than most of us who do. He also keeps up on his neighbors' comings and goings while shying away from gossip, which is how the peace is kept in these small rural communities, although I thought I detected the occasional glimmer of juicy untold stories.

Erik knows everyone hereabouts, partly because there aren't that many to know. The nearest town of Melrose consists of two bars, a fly shop, an old brick hotel, and a handful of houses, and boasts a population of 125. But at what amounts to rush hour, when the bars are open and guided trips are returning to the shop, you might see all of fifteen people. Of course, Erik knows the owners of the fly shop and instinctively understands their business. Like ranching, the profits are seasonal, but the work is year-round and the milling fishermen they wrangle each morning bear a strong resemblance to livestock.

Erik started off raising cattle here on the ranch where he was born, later switching to sheep for economic reasons. I was tempted to ask if cattlemen still refer to sheep as "range maggots," but decided against it. John Updike said it's useful for a writer to know people who know things, and part of that equation involves staying quiet and listening, contributing only enough to the conversation to avoid seeming dim-witted.

There was less reminiscing than I expected between Mike and Erik, and I think I know why, having gone down the same rabbit hole myself. Even just an hour of dredging up old times and old loves with a former friend can leave you longing for the malleable present, where possibilities still exist. The stark contrast between then and now can be disorienting. It's like thinking you've spotted an old girlfriend in a crowd, but even as your right brain says *That's her!* the left brain reasonably answers, *Nope, if anything, that would have to be her granddaughter.*

After the Big Hole, we fished a little creek that we're forbidden to mention the name or location of. We drove for a while on county roads, stopped for coffee in a town large enough to have stoplights, and turned up an unpaved road that ran through miles of empty rangeland. We passed a black-on-yellow Highway Department sign peppered with bullet holes but still legible enough to read, ROAD NOT MAINTAINED FOR WINTER TRAVEL, briefly mistook a scrap of black garbage bag fluttering in the breeze for a raven, and began to climb through rolling foothills as the valley around us narrowed. At the top of one rise we surprised a small herd of pronghorns that bolted parallel to the road and Mike accelerated to keep up. We clocked them at a sustained 45 miles an hour before they peeled off.

We'd been roughly following the creek for miles, but it was concealed by an unbroken fringe of willows snaking across open prairie. When we finally crossed it, I could see how small it was. Where we pulled off the road, it was no wider in places than my 7-foot, 9-inch fly rod was long, but it had fishy undercut banks and deep corner pools at the bends.

Few tourists would bother with a creek this small even if they knew about it, and locals would only bring their kids here because it's too shallow to drown in, so the brook trout were fat, wild, and heartbreakingly gullible. Trout that have been fished for smell a rat when your fly drags on the water, but these trout just thought it was getting away and would chase it down—another reason to bring a kid here.

The better trout were in the 10-inch range, and although Mike and I have caught larger brook trout in eastern Canada, we've lived in the Mountain West long enough for a 10-inch brookie to be a fine fish, so we decided to string some up for dinner that night.

In these complicated times it's possible to lose track of what fishing is about until the familiar ritual cuts through the ambiguity: the killing blow with the knife handle, the incision from vent to chin, the guts and gills that come out in a single, bloodless piece, the stripping of the mud vein along the spine with a thumbnail, and the quick rinse in creek water. That little twinge of sadness you feel when the light goes out is no more than the acknowledgment that everything edible was once alive, and when I showed my snapshots of that trip to friends back home, it was the still life of brook trout browning in a flying pan that they lingered over the longest.

Back at the car, Mike said he had first fished this creek at age ten and it hadn't changed a bit—not something you hear often—adding, in a matter-of-fact way, "I wouldn't be surprised to see my dad walk over right now and ask me how I did." Mike is a photographer by trade and he was currently working on a book that will compare how this region is now versus how it was when he grew up here, so although the nostalgia wasn't overwhelming, it was in the air like background radiation.

One day we drove far up the Big Hole to where the river was creek-sized and wadable, meandering across a wide, willowy valley ringed with mountains under a turquoise sky—a real Montana postcard. But the temperature was already in the 90s, presaging the 2021 drought. (They're so common now you have to date them.) The river wasn't in a generous mood, but we still managed to catch a few small brookies and I landed a grayling that made my day. The fish wasn't especially large, but grayling are native to the Big Hole and the river is now their last indigenous holdout in the state, so catching one is like finding an arrowhead.

One day we went back to Mike's little brook trout creek and got in lower down where it was fenced off with freshly treated wood posts and shiny new barbed wire strung tighter than banjo strings. It looked forbiddingly private but was, in fact, a Bureau of Land Management grazing lease, so we had every right to be there. That's what I planned to tell anyone who asked, but no one ever did. During that entire day, only one pickup passed on the road and the driver smiled and waved without slowing down, acknowledging that fishing for brook trout was more fun than whatever he was doing. I had watched the guy coming up the valley for the last ten minutes, towing a wake of gray dust, and realized that if you wanted to sneak up on someone here, you wouldn't do it in a pickup.

We had split up to fish the creek and Buncie mostly stayed with Mike (they're already inseparable) but now and then, on his own schedule, he would barrel over to say hello to me and Dan, tongue lolling, ears flapping like wings, oblivious of things like fly rods, lines, and hooks and just generally delighted to be alive and young. Buncie will slow down and wise up in time, but at this stage he's as elastically goofy as a cartoon character and always good for a laugh.

Dan left the next morning on his long drive back to South Dakota and that afternoon Mike and I found ourselves parked on a bench of land above a meadow stream, eating lunch and watching through binoculare as a trout rose to a sparse Pale Morning Dun hatch in the bend below. Higher up the drainage this had been a mountain freestone stream, but down here where the valley widened, it spread out into looping meanders, picked up groundwater seeps, and began to look distinctly spring-creeky, with mats of vegetation waving languidly in the slow current. This was late in the trip, when things were winding down, so we took our time finishing our sandwiches before ambling down to the water, where Mike left me to it and walked up to the next bend with Buncie at his heels.

I tied on a size 16 PMD and tried it out on one of the smaller fish. He glanced at it on two successive casts, but didn't take, so I added a size 18 Pheasant Tail on a dropper and he ate that on the first drift. It was a chubby 10-inch cuttbow that I landed quickly.

Now that I thought I had the right fly, I wanted to try for the bigger fish that was rising upstream in a smooth current on the outside of a weed bed. There was an afternoon breeze gusting, and I thought I would get a better drift if I waded out close to the edge of the weeds to make my cast, but a few yards off the bank I sank in the deep, black muck that had accumulated on the inside of the bend and was quickly stuck as securely as a bridge piling while my hip boots filled with water. Two things occurred to me: that this was a beginner's mistake that I would have seen coming if I hadn't been in a fish trance, and that in slightly different circumstances it could be the first step in the long, slow process of fossilization.

If you've ever had to extricate yourself from this fix, you'll know that the process of getting one foot loose inevitably gets the other foot stuck more securely and progress is so agonizingly slow that your predicament soon takes on the proportions of an existential crisis. It didn't help that sometime during the struggle the wind blew my hat off and I stood there forlornly watching it drift downstream.

When I finally got myself out, I sat on the bank for a minute—breathless and embarrassed—then emptied my hip boots, trudged downstream to retrieve my hat from where it had washed up on the outside of a bend like flotsam from a shipwreck, and marched back with all the casual dignity I could muster.

I hooked the big fish on the Pheasant Tail by making a single long cast from the bank, carefully played him out in open water until I got his head up, and slid him neatly over the weeds to my feet. When we had first seen him through binoculars, we guessed him at around 20 inches and we were right, but it was a 20-inch whitefish. Not something I'd have gone to any trouble to catch.

Working on up that bank, I got two more nice cuttbows, then waded out to a small, grassy island—being careful to stay on gravel bottom—and caught a third that I'd seen rising on the far side. When I turned to wade back after releasing it, I found Mike standing on the bank with Buncie at his feet, chewing on a stick he had found. No telling how long they'd been there.

I was leaving the next day, but Mike would be staying on for a while to bear down on his project without having fishing friends underfoot. As it turned out, he'd fish one more creek that he had first fished with his dad and later he'd text me a photo of a fat, beautifully colored 20-inch brown trout that was exactly the fish I'd envisioned when I was casting to that whitefish.

That last night at the ranch, I had a vivid dream about kissing a girl when I was sixteen. Not any specific girl, but a strangely recognizable composite that my sleeping mind conjured out of all the girls I ever loved, or thought I did, or wished I had, giving it plenty to work with. Whoever she was, we had wandered away from a party and talked for hours under a big sky with a bazillion stars until a spark was struck and nature took its normal teenage course.

But through the odd logic of dreams, I was also a composite: unquestionably sixteen, but also somehow my current age of seventy-four, with a lifetime's worth of adult hindsight and regrets, so this time I could be patient and considerate instead of just one-dimensionally horny, as I surely was back then.

That's it—nothing profound, and totally G-rated—but I woke the next morning thinking, *Well, it was only a dream, but for a minute there it seemed like I actually knew then what I know now.* Then I snagged a ride to the airport and flew home.

John Gierach's Fly-fishing Library

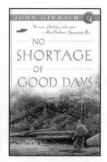

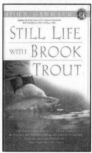

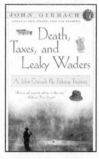

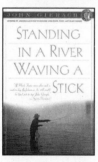
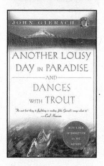
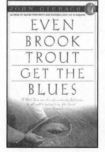

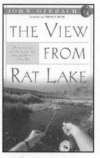

"The next best
thing to
fly-fishing
is reading
John Gierach's
essays about it."

—Carl Hiaasen

Available wherever books are sold or at SimonandSchuster.com

SIMON &
SCHUSTER